PRAISE FOR
Adopted, Returned, Unwanted
...My Foster Care Journey

"In life, everyone will face some form of trials, tribulations, and defeat. This memoir is a story of triumph and perseverance. As a person who never gives up, I can resonate with Judy's life story. Her courage, resilience, and faith led her to find the truth 40 years later. As a certified respite foster parent, I endorse this book and believe others who were connected to the foster care system would benefit from it as well."

Omarosa Manigault Newman
New York Times #1 Best Selling Author

"Adopted, **Returned**, Unwanted...My Foster Care Journey... takes readers on a journey of real lived experiences that many Americans live through, but choose not to share. The journey is at times dark, but rich while experiencing foster care and triumphantly heals and succeeds in life as an adult. I believe this is a great motivational and inspirational masterpiece that everyone can get lost in and leave the hopeful, smiling, and proud Judy!"

Dr. Nyree Berry
Former sociology college professor of Judy Levisy

ADOPTED, RETURNED, UNWANTED

...My Foster Care Journey

ADOPTED, RETURNED, UNWANTED

...My Foster Care Journey

Judith Levisy

Jule Book Publishing

Los Angeles, California

ADOPTED, RETURNED, UNWANTED
...My Foster Care Journey

Published by
Jule Book Publishing
Los Angeles, California
judylevisy@gmail.com

Judith Levisy, Publisher / Editorial Director
Yvonne Rose/Quality Press.info, Book Packager
Cover Photo - Courtesy of Airic Lewis of Nirvana Studios, Hollywood

ALL RIGHTS RESERVED

No part of this book may be reproduced or transmitted in any form or by any means electronic or mechanical, including photocopying, recording, or by any information storage and retrieval system without written permission from the authors, except for the inclusion of brief quotations in a review.

DISCLAIMER

This work depicts actual events in the life of the author as truthfully as recollection permits. While all persons within are actual individuals, names and identifying characteristics have been changed to respect their privacy.

Dedication

My first dedication is to GOD for loving me, when no one else did. I give HIM all the Praise, Glory, and Honor for giving me the courage and strength to stand in the midst of adversity. Through it all, I had to learn to trust in HIM.

To my foster siblings who endured the same heartfelt pain, mental and physical abuse, and abandonment. We made it through, despite never being loved; but we continue to love one another.

To all the children that were abandoned and placed in foster or group homes. You do not have to be a victim of your environment. You do not have to be a victim of your parents' decisions. You can live out your goals and dreams. You can be and do what others have told you throughout your life that you cannot do. You were not a mistake. GOD placed you here for a purpose.

To my sons, I thank you for showing me how much you love and appreciate me as your mother. You will always be the wind beneath my wings; and as our family continues to grow, our love continues to expand. We have a family bond that only grows stronger.

Lastly, to my foster parents. I can only say thank you for feeding, clothing, and housing me. You stepped in when my biological parents stepped away.

I made it through. I did not lose!!!

Foreword

I am delighted that the world is about to meet its next best-selling author in the person of Judy Levisy. From the first day my wife introduced us in Encino, California, to this day, Judy has remained one of the most energetic, exciting, and expressive people we know. Judy loves life, she loves people, and she lives fully.

Judy's decision to share this MEMOIR is a vision whose time has come. This story ends happily because she made it out alive. But she didn't just survive. This memoir proves that she does thrive. The title alone reads like a "Lifetime" movie. I sincerely desire this book to heal many hurting hearts, minds, and souls.

What excites me the most is that I met Judy decades after her foster care debacle. My wife and I get to do life with her in ministry and business. We've been fortunate to have a front-row view of her life and how God has turned her tragedy into triumph. She's a fantastic example of what defying the gravitational pull of adverse circumstances and overcoming the odds look like.

She does not act, look, or sound like what she's been through. She is a loving mother, grandmother, and a consistent and loyal friend. As you read her story, I hope places of hurt, pain, and trauma in your life that occurred at other people's hands will begin to heal. It is often said that hurting people hurt people. I concur that healed people help people. The title of this book merely chronicles the journey that has brought her to her present state of being Accepted, Received, and Un-scathed. Ladies and Gentlemen, we present the newly published author, Judy Levisy.

Dr. Desmond Pringle, Pastor
The Watered Garden Christian Fellowship

Contents

Introduction

Adopted, **Returned**, Unwanted… **My Foster Care Journey** is the story of my life in foster care, along with six other foster children. The book gives you an inside view of the good, the bad, the ugly events, circumstances, and lifestyles, including mental and physical abuse.

I was born in May 1961 in Buffalo, New York. Miscegenation was still illegal in twenty-two states in 1960. The word miscegenation comes from the Latin words misère (to mix) and genus (type, family, or descent) and has been used to refer to cohabitation or intermarriage between racial groups. Regulated by state law, miscegenation was illegal in many states for decades. New York was 1 of 9 states that never had Anti-Miscegenation Laws. In the other states, all bi-racial children born to a white and Black couple were said to be illegitimate. Bi-racial children were often shunned and put in orphanages because of the attacks from both Black and white people alike. They were born unwanted or in some cases, their mother was single or incredibly young, and poor.

I looked white on the day I was born. I was told I had white skin, blonde hair, and blue eyes and my mother had given me to a Caucasian couple that wanted to adopt me. Living with my newfound parents did not last long. My skin, hair, and eyes started turning colors when I was six months old. That's when my new parents realized they were lied to, and their new baby daughter was not 100% Caucasian. They returned me to the adoption agency. I was eight months old when the orphanage placed me with Lloyd and Gertrude, who lived at 17 Viola Park.

My foster parents never wanted any of us to know our background or find our biological family. But when I was able to understand what it meant to be a foster child, my curiosity grew. I remember asking my foster mother, on many occasions, about my biological mother and father. She would always try to avoid my questions or sometimes say that my mother was white and was unable to keep me.

1

My Biological Parents

My biological mother, Judith (Judy) Mary Levisy, was born in January 1943 to Harry and Marie Levisy in Buffalo, New York.

I learned later that my mother's father was half-black. According to the 1920 Census, his father was a Caucasian, and his mother Mary Levisy, a Black woman, was born in Virginia in 1876. Harry was a musician and played the guitar. Marie was born in 1917 to Albert and Mary Wagner. Harry and Marie met one day while she was sitting on her porch. Harry noticed her as he was passing by. They started conversing and the rest became history. They had two children, Harold and Judith (Judy).

Judy was an overly ambitious young girl who stayed to herself in school. She felt she was accepted more by white people, even though her father was partially Black. Judy was sixteen years old when she met seventeen-year-old Jozelle (Billy) Carter. She would leave the house to go watch him play with a well-known band at the nearby clubs. She loved to dance, and she sang in her school chorus.

My foster mother said she never knew anything about my father. She also said that if I tried searching for my parents, I could upset either one of them and they may continue to reject me.

It was in September 1983 when I was finally able to search for and meet my biological mother. I was 22 years old when I saw my birth certificate for the first time. It was given to me by my Navy recruiting officer after I explained to him that I was a foster child and had no idea who my parents were. It seemed he was eager to find out, as much as I was. We read it together and it showed that I was named after my mother who is white, but the space for my father was left blank. At that moment I didn't care because all I could think of was the fact that I was holding my first piece of evidence containing half of my real identity.

I remember leaving the recruiting office all excited with my birth certificate in hand. When I arrived home, I told my foster mother I had it and asked her if she knew that I was named after my mother. She said yes and began to tell me what I had been asking her for years. She said I came to her and Lloyd from the orphanage in February 1962, wearing a pink bunny snowsuit. She explained that when I was 7 years old, she remembered reading the obituaries in The Buffalo News and came across the name Harry C. Levisy. Gertrude said she wanted to find out more information, so she contacted the Edwards Funeral Home where the funeral was held. They told her that Harry's funeral had been the day before. Apparently, she wanted to go and see my biological family. *I never knew this.*

After she explained all that to me, I grabbed the telephone book and searched for anyone with the Levisy name. I came across two people. One listing was my name because I helped my foster sister Diane get a phone for her household. The other listing was for Harold Levisy. I was nervous as I dialed the listed number. A little girl answered the phone with a bright voice saying 'hello.' I asked her if I could talk to her mother or father, and she said they were not home, and she was by herself. She then said her grandmother was home. I asked her what her name was, and she said, "Robyn" and asked me if I wanted to talk to her grandmother. I said yes.

When her grandmother said, 'hello,' I said 'hello' and told her my name. I shared everything I knew with her about my birth certificate and what I had just learned from my foster mother about my grandfather Harry, who was her husband. While I was explaining she never said a word. When I finished, I asked her, "Does any of this sound familiar to you?" She said, "Yes it does." I then said, "So I can be talking to my grandmother?" She replied, "You are talking to your grandmother!" She told me her name was Marie.

I cannot explain how I was feeling at that moment. I became overwhelmed with excitement to finally know something about my real life. My grandmother began to tell me about my mother. She said she was at work and would have her call me. I asked for her number, and she said my mom started a new job and it would be best if I waited for her to call me when she got off work. I gave her my phone number and she said she would give it to her. I assumed she did not want to give me her number because she needed to break the news to Judy herself.

I was able to answer the phone when Judy called later that afternoon. My emotions were everywhere. I was nervous, excited, and scared, all at the same time. I said, "Hello." She said, "Hello, my name is Judy, and I am not sure who to ask for." I said, "It's me. My name is Judy too." She asked me how I was doing. I explained my nervousness to her. She said she felt the same way. She wanted to know if she and my grandmother would be able to visit me later that evening. I asked Gertrude if it would be okay and she said, "Yes, but we have to go to the laundromat first and they can come over when we get back."

They arrived at our place at 10880 Erie Road, around 7 p.m. At the time, we were living in a motor home as a result of a fire that destroyed the family home when another young foster child lit a match in the basement. When they arrived, I remember being so scared and nervous that I hid behind a box full of clothes. Gertrude said, "Don't be nervous, this is what you wanted." She greeted my newfound family at the door and invited them in. Lloyd was in the motor home with my 3-month-old son, Jeffrey. When Judy and Marie came in, all I could do was stare at them. I was speechless. Her first words were, "You look just like your father." At that moment I felt she would be able to tell me about him, as well.

My mother and I kept staring at each other. Then she introduced Marie and said, "This is your grandmother." Judy started telling me about the rest of her family. She said she was married and had two other children. She showed me pictures of 2-year-old Julie and 7-year-old Joey. She then said, "I know you want to know why I gave you up for adoption," and began to explain. "I was young, only seventeen when I got pregnant, and my father told me I could not keep you. I had to give you away. I knew you would be better off with an adopted family." She said that she and Marie picked out the adoption agency, as well as the couple who wanted to adopt me. They had chosen a white family, whose father was a Dentist. She felt they would be able to take better care of me and give me a life she was unable to.

She expressed how happy she was to see how well I was doing. Gertrude asked her if she felt they did a good job raising me. She replied with a cheerful, "Yes!" She then dropped the bomb and all my good feelings fell to the floor. Judy started telling me more about her married life. She said she told her husband about me and asked his permission to come over. She then said, "This will be the only time I can see you and talk to you because I am married to a Polish guy from Dunkirk, and Polish People in Dunkirk are very prejudiced." She went on to say, "It would be hard for me to explain a 22-year-old Black daughter to his Polish family." As she was telling me this, I could feel my heart and stomach start to fall and hit the floor. All the joy I was feeling for finally knowing some truth had suddenly vanished with her hurtful words. I wanted to cry, but I could not. I knew they could see my displeasure. Gertrude had a look on her face as if to say, "I told you so." I felt that Judy did not want anything to do with me. I just listened to her and was finally able to change the subject.

I started asking her questions regarding my father. I wanted to know why his name was not on my birth certificate. She said his name was Billy and he was playing the drums for Grover Washington Jr when they first met. She told me how she would sneak out of the house to go watch him play at the different clubs. When I asked for his last name, she said she did not remember. I asked her if she knew where he might be living or how I would be able to contact him. She said she had no idea. I felt she did know but did not want to tell me for fear of him coming back into her life. She said she found out he had other girls pregnant at the same time she was pregnant with me. She also said he is probably dead by now due to his heavy drug use, and looking for him would be a waste of my time. Her saying this further piqued my interest in finding my father and starting a relationship with him. I became further inquisitive since my mother apparently wanted to continue to act like I did not exist. She did say, "He lived with his aunt, so that should tell you something about him. He was not a good person." I was a little confused by her comment.

Our conversation lasted for about two hours. After they left, I felt a little better, knowing something about my biological family. But it truly hurt knowing that I was still unwanted by her, which put me on a journey to find my biological father.

2

The Colbert Family

Lloyd and Gertrude Colbert

Before my arrival, the orphanage had already placed Melvin, Loretta, and Margaret, three bi-racial children in their home. It was a cold winter day in February 1962 when I was placed in their foster home. I was 8 months old when I arrived at their 2-story yellow house on 17 Viola Park, dressed in a pink bunny snowsuit. Gertrude later told me I was the prettiest thing she had ever seen.

Lloyd was a tall dark-skinned African American born in Halifax, Virginia in September 1927, to Flora Murphy and William Colbert. He was raised by his grandmother, Flora, and was led to believe that she was his biological mother. He was also raised with his biological mother and was led to believe that she was his sister. We, as children, called his mother, Aunt Flora, and his grandmother, Grandma Flora. Lloyd discovered the truth at the age of seventy when his sister/mother passed away. He also had a brother named Benjamin, whom we called Uncle Ben.

Aunt Flora was married to Uncle George. Uncle Ben was married to Aunt Phyllis. These were the only aunts and uncles we knew about growing up.

Lloyd had moved to Buffalo at an early age with his mother, sister, and other relatives. He served in the United States Army and Navy. He retired from working as a Heavy Equipment Operator for the City of Buffalo where he had worked for 30 years.

Gertrude was of medium complexion, born in Pensacola, Florida in October 1930. Gertrude's mother, Esther, was only 14 years old when she was born. Gertrude was an only child and was eventually sent away to boarding school in North Carolina.

Gertrude and Lloyd were married in November 1954, in Buffalo, New York. Two years later, they had a daughter, Diane Colbert, who was born in July 1956.

After realizing that Gertrude could not have more children, the Colberts decided to adopt so they would have a large family and their children could take care of them in their old age. However, when they were informed that all state funds would cease once the adoption was finalized, they changed their minds and became a foster home in order to keep the monthly payments flowing in.

Diane Colbert

Diane was treated much better than her foster siblings. She always had her own bedroom, while Loretta, Margaret, and I had to share. Diane was never held to the same house rules as her foster siblings, and therefore she never received discipline for having a dirty room or for not making up her bed. She never had any chores either. Diane always had the finest of clothes, while her foster siblings wore clothes from Goodwill or hand-me-downs given to Gertrude by her friends. Gertrude paid for Diane to take piano lessons, which enabled her to become a good pianist.

Diane never had to work, but when her foster siblings turned twelve years old they were forced to work in the fields alongside migrant workers.

3

The Foster Children

Through the years, Lloyd and Gertrude took in twenty-three foster children. Gertrude had decided that they were not going to accept any child over the age of five.

Some of them lived with us for a few weeks or a few months; but none of them were raised in the Colberts' home like the children mentioned below.

Lloyd and Gertrude played a significant role in all of the misfortunes that occurred during my childhood. *I never understood why two black people who hated white people as much as they did would want to raise half-white children.*

Melvin

Melvin is said to be Italian and Black, born in February 1958. He was only 17 months old when he was given to the Colberts by his biological father who was taking care of him, but for some unfortunate reason was unable to anymore, even though he was financially well off. Melvin was the first foster child that Lloyd and Gertrude had considered adopting, but changed their minds when the adoption agency informed them that they would no longer receive state funding once the adoption was finalized.

Melvin was a very smart curly-haired little boy who grew into an intelligent young man. He believed that people must work for what they wanted in life. Melvin did exactly that. He always worked several jobs at a time. He graduated from Lake Shore High in 1977 and attended Alfred State College, majoring in Construction. Melvin was still living in the Colberts' foster home when he graduated from college in 1980.

Melvin was the oldest of the foster children and endured a lot of physical, mental, and verbal abuse. The abuse became more intense and extreme as he grew older. He was the first to start working in the fields alongside the migrant workers. It did not matter to Gertrude if it was inclement weather or if the sun was too hot… she wanted the money.

Melvin was always loyal to Lloyd and Gertrude, even during the abuse. He felt obligated to give her what she asked for or took from him. I remember so vividly how Melvin worked his butt off and she took all his money. At one point, Melvin was working three jobs. He worked at a gas station and had two construction jobs. Gertrude knew when he was getting paid and took his money every time. He worked the third job to have money for himself.

I remember numerous beatings Melvin received, for no reason at all. In one of the houses we lived in, there was a room near the back door that held all the cookware and canned goods that Gertrude used for her catering business. One day, Gertrude was upset with Melvin and started hitting him and pushing him into the pots, which fell on him. Lloyd came downstairs, picked him up, and started throwing him up against those metal and iron pots, all because of his money. Melvin sustained many bruises and cuts.

The abuse Melvin endured on the day that he refused to give up his third check will forever be etched in my mind. He had already given her his first and second checks. I remember the day when he came home from working his third job, she told him to give her his money and he said, "No." Gertrude then told him she was going to put him out if he didn't and he said, he would sleep in his car. I could see the anger build up on Gertrude's face when Melvin began standing up for himself, which was something she was not used to him doing. She then told him in a loud voice that she would flatten his tires.

I remember the beating she gave him with her balled fist and when she got tired, she called on Lloyd who came downstairs and began hitting him with the belt that he had pulled out of his pants. Lloyd always took her side without knowing the truth. I could not believe what I was witnessing. As I stood there watching in horror, I was asking myself, *would I have to suffer like him?*

Melvin ended up leaving that night in his car. I was so glad he left to stay with people who really loved and believed in him. Melvin is happily married to Sydney and living in Chesapeake, Virginia.

Samuel (Sam) and Loretta

Sam, who was born on February 6, 1957, and Loretta, who was born on January 21, 1959, are siblings. Their mother, Marie Falzone, was of Italian descent. Their father was African American. Loretta was three years old, and Sam was five years old when the Orphanage placed them with Lloyd and Gertrude in 1962. Loretta and Sam were suffering from starvation when they arrived. She remembers eating everything that was placed before her. As a child, Loretta used to suck her pinkie finger. Gertrude would put tape and hot sauce on her finger to prevent her from doing so.

Sam, who must have suffered a tremendous amount of abuse, was returned to the Orphanage two years later. Lloyd and Gertrude were not able, nor mentally prepared to handle Sam's anxiety or his mental state of mind; so, they gave him back but decided to keep Loretta. The separation from his only sibling caused even more anxiety throughout the years. Sam passed away in January 2016.

Growing up, Loretta was always a little bigger than Margaret and me. Gertrude always called her big-boned, an ox, or a horse. I remember so many times how Gertrude would punch Loretta in her back with the ball of her fist. She would always punch Loretta until she fell to the floor. Then sometimes Gertrude would bend over Loretta and continue to punch her, and she often kicked her as well. There are two main instances that I remember so vividly as if they happened yesterday. Gertrude and

Diane, to this very day, said it never happened; but I needed to address these two vicious and abusive attacks because they **DID**.

We were living on Maiden Lane. Loretta was around 11 years old, and she did something wrong, according to Gertrude. Gertrude punched her several times in her back, as usual, and she fell to the floor. Gertrude then raised her foot and kicked Loretta between her legs. Loretta started screaming with terror, got up off the floor, and ran to the bathroom. She saw blood coming down her legs. Loretta opened the door, still crying and telling Gertrude she was bleeding. Gertrude told Diane to go check on her, and said, "She probably started her period." I felt Loretta's pain that day and wondered if it would happen to me.

The second vicious and abusive attack occurred about a year later at 10880 Erie Road. It was a late summer evening when Gertrude started arguing with Loretta again. Everybody was home at the time. Gertrude began yelling and punching Loretta very hard in her back, as usual. Loretta fell to the floor and was having difficulty breathing. I remember looking at her lying in the middle of the doorway, halfway in the house, and halfway out the front door. Her upper torso was on the porch. She was gasping for air and Gertrude still punched her. (*I am crying right now. This is so hard to write, but I must.*) Lloyd stepped in and told Gertrude to stop. Lloyd began to give Loretta CPR, while someone else called 911. The Paramedics came, examined her, and said she was going to be fine. No one told them Gertrude had beaten her, just before they arrived. To my surprise, they did nothing. Loretta went to bed, beaten, and bruised, while

Gertrude carried on as if everything was normal. Loretta and I talked about that incident years later. She explained to me how she faked her passing out because she thought it would stop Gertrude from beating her.

Loretta was also forced to work in the fields when she turned twelve. All Loretta's money went to Gertrude who had become very friendly with the M&T Bank personnel in Angola, which allowed her to sign and deposit our checks into her account.

In 1977 Gertrude entered Loretta in the Debutante Pageant and she won First Runner-Up. Loretta graduated from Lake Shore High that same year. Loretta felt that she was not ready for college, but Gertrude forced her to go because she knew she would still receive money from the State. She attended Alfred University for a semester before joining the U.S. Navy on May 19, 1978.

Loretta and her husband Mitch were living in Virginia Beach when she retired from the Navy in 2002, as a Yeoman Chief. She served our Country for 23 years. Loretta is currently living a happy and prosperous life in Las Vegas.

Despite all she endured at the hands of her abusers, Loretta felt she needed to be obligated to Lloyd and Gertrude to a certain extent. Her attitude towards Gertrude has since changed.

Margaret

Margaret, born April 9, 1961, is said to be Irish and Black. She has straight brown hair. Margaret was three years old when the Orphanage placed her with the Colberts in the Summer of

1964. Margaret and I were only 46 days apart in age and were often asked if we were twins. Margaret and I were the closest of all the children. She always wanted a middle name, so she named herself Margaret Rochelle. Her favorite color has always been yellow.

She began to display mischievous behavior at a young age. She stole money out of her third-grade teacher, Mrs. Christopher's desk, and refused to tell the truth. Margaret was 12 years old when she started smoking cigarettes. She used to take them from our grandmother, Esther's, purse. I remember one time when one of Esther's close friends was visiting her along with her granddaughter. Margaret saw an opportunity to take a cigarette out of the pack that Esther had set on the table near her ashtray. The three of us - Margaret, Esther's friend's granddaughter, and I – ran out of the house to the chicken coup with the cigarette and the matches. Esther's granddaughter convinced us to try it with her. Margaret took the first puff and started choking right away! I was so scared for her and knew I did not want to get caught so I ran off. I never did that again and did my best to warn her that smoking was a bad thing.

Margaret was also twelve when she was forced to work in the fields and she had to give Gertrude all her money, as well. We worked alongside each other digging potatoes and picking strawberries.

Gertrude eventually found out about her smoking when the school principal called to say that he caught Margaret and a few other girls smoking outside the school. After the principal called her, Gertrude went to the store and bought a pack of Camel cigarettes and when Margaret came home from school, she made her eat the entire pack of cigarettes. Gertrude forced Margaret to eat Camel cigarettes because they did not have a filter and the taste was nasty. The tobacco made Margaret sick, and Gertrude stood over her with a belt or switch and hit her every time she spit them out from choking. Gertrude forced her to eat cigarettes several times because she thought and felt that forcing her to eat them would teach her a lesson and cause her not to smoke again. I believe she picked up the habit of smoking from our grandmother, Esther.

Margaret was in seventh grade when she took a girl's purse out of her gym locker. The principal called Gertrude, and Margaret was beaten with switches without any clothes on and forced to sit in the bathtub filled with cold water, to keep her body from swelling up. A few days later, when everyone was leaving to catch the school bus, Gertrude told Margaret she was not going to school. When I returned home, Margaret was gone. Gertrude sent her away to a girls' home somewhere in Buffalo. She said she did it to save me. Gertrude would never tell me where she was, but I eventually found out and used to go see her whenever I went to choir rehearsal. It was our little secret. Margaret stayed in that girls' home for about two years.

It was the summer of 1976 when Lloyd and Gertrude planned a family road trip to Florida so Gertrude could meet a sister whom she never knew she had. I begged Gertrude to allow Margaret to go with us and to my surprise, she said yes. The two of us had so much fun being together again. But Gertrude said it was the worst trip the family ever took, because of us. I was not sure what she meant because we did nothing wrong. I still believe to this day, Gertrude did not like the bond we shared. It seemed our happiness made her even more bitter!

After I left for college, Margaret eventually moved back in with Lloyd and Gertrude. One summer night in 1981 Margaret met Walter (Walt) Postell at Mickey Rats Beach Club. They eventually got together and had two daughters. Margaret had a very rough life, which caused us to lose contact with each other for more than 30 years.

Corey

Corey, born in March 1964, is said to be West Indies and Black. He was only 4 days old when the Orphanage placed him in the home. He was the darkest of all the named children and was treated much better because of his skin color. He was a heavy bedwetter and would wet the bed every night. Each time he did, Gertrude would make him take his wet sheets outside and shake them until they were dry. We used to laugh at him because that was the only form of punishment he received.

Despite his bedwetting, he was ALWAYS Gertrude's favorite, and she did not hide it. It was as if she was his biological mother. Whatever Corey needed or wanted, she made sure he had it. Corey was the tallest of all the foster children. He ran track and played football and basketball throughout his middle and high school years. Melvin would frequently tell them that Corey was good and was going to make it to the NBA if he continued to practice and play in school. One day Melvin told Lloyd and Gertrude that Corey needed the best basketball shoes, which, at that time, were the Converse All-Star sneakers. Gertrude made sure Corey got them. But when Alan needed new sneakers, she refused to buy him any and told him, "You only want them because Corey has them." No, his feet were growing, and he needed new shoes, as well. Corey never had to work in the fields with the rest of his foster siblings.

He graduated from Lake Shore High in 1983 and went on to pursue a degree from Cortland University where he met his first wife. In the beginning, Lloyd refused to go to the wedding because she was white, but Gertrude convinced him to attend. They had two children. Corey never made it to the NBA; instead, he became a coach for a school district near Buffalo.

Alan

Alan, born in April 1966, is the only all-Black foster child out of the original seven. He was five years old when he was placed with Lloyd and Gertrude on a cold winter day in February 1971. Alan, along with a few of his siblings were found abandoned in a home with no food, heat, or water. He had to be carried from the car to the house due to the deep snow that he had never seen before. Alan had a habit of sucking his thumb and Gertrude would tape it like she did with Loretta. At times she would often dip his finger in hot sauce.

It was said that he was related to Lloyd's side of the family, which explains why he was treated so badly. Gertrude hated her in-laws, and they knew it. There was a particular incident that Alan reminded me of when Gertrude would have killed him if Lloyd had not returned home from work early. He was just seven years old and in second grade at Farnham Elementary. His class was going on a field trip to the Buffalo Zoo, and he reminded Gertrude that he needed $2 to pay for the trip. We were living at 363 Maiden Lane and the school bus would always drive past our house first, to pick up the children at the end of the road. We knew that once the bus passed our house, we had about three minutes before it came back down the road to pick us up. Alan kept telling Gertrude that the bus was coming and that he needed the money. Gertrude was upstairs and completely ignored him because she did not want to give the money to him. He saw her purse sitting on the table and took what he thought was a $2 bill but turned out to be a $20 bill. While shopping at the souvenir shop getting Gertrude a gift, the cashier gave him back more money and he thought she made a mistake. It was also his teacher's birthday, so he wrapped a $5 bill in a napkin and gave it to her as a birthday gift. When the teacher and the class returned from the Zoo, the teacher told the principal what occurred, and the principal called Gertrude. She went to the school to get him and the money. When they returned home, all hell broke loose.

Gertrude made Alan take off his clothes and go into the bathroom. She had Lloyd's thick motorcycle belt, which she had cut the ends off to look like several belts in one. She proceeded to beat Alan and continued to beat him, even while his blood was splattering on the ceiling, walls, and floor. Lloyd came home early from work and heard Alan screaming and when he opened the bathroom door, he saw his blood everywhere and started yelling at Gertrude. To this day, Alan will tell you that if Lloyd had not come home early, he would have died that day. Gertrude tried to kill him over $20, and he was only seven years old.

Alan was always smart and learned a lot from Melvin. Alan knew what he wanted to do when he grew up, and despite the mental and physical abuse he endured, he always remained optimistic about fulfilling his dream. In 1982 Alan was on the Varsity track team, along with Corey. He graduated from Lake Shore High in 1984.

In 1986, when I returned home from serving overseas, I stayed with Lloyd and Gertrude on Detroit Street in Farnham. They were renting a small garage apartment from a friend which was a far cry from what they were used to.

Alan was the only foster child still living with them. I remember one particular day, when he came in from working all night as a DJ, Gertrude wanted him to wash the dishes. I could not understand why, when she could clearly see that I was already cleaning the kitchen. Alan wanted to sleep, but she kept yelling at him and threatening to put him out if he did not take over the task of washing the dishes. I continued to help him anyway. He still lived with them after I moved away with my husband and two sons.

In early 1988, Gertrude and Lloyd moved to Virginia, chasing after who they thought was her rich uncle. They left Alan alone in the apartment and never told him they were moving. He thought they were going on a trip. Gertrude had Diane take him some food and pick up her state check once a month. Diane went along with the scheme and never told him they were not coming back. She eventually, under Gertrude's instructions, had the utilities disconnected and no longer took him anything to eat, even though Alan was in college and Gertrude was still receiving state funds.

Alan followed his dreams and goals by becoming a well-known DJ in Buffalo.

4

Judith Mary Levisy - My Story

I, Judith Mary Levisy, was born to a partially white mother, age 17, and an 18-year-old Black father on May 25, 1961. My parents were extremely young, and my father deserted her when he found out she was pregnant. On the day I was born, my mother's father told her not to bring a baby back home. My mother and grandmother, with the help of an adoption agency, selected a white couple who they thought would be my perfect parents. The father was a well-off dentist, so they thought this new couple would be able to provide a life for me that my mother felt she was unable to.

My new parents were excited to adopt who they thought was a pure white baby girl with blonde hair and blue eyes. (My foster mother told me I was born with blonde hair, blue eyes, and white skin.) Six months later the adoption became null when my eyes, skin, and hair started turning darker. They realized I was not who they wanted. I was returned to the agency and placed in an orphanage. My new parents took back the name they had given me and had it erased from my birth certificate. I ended up in an orphanage as a nameless six-month-old baby girl. It was the orphanage staff that decided to name me after my biological mother. I was eight months old when they placed me in the foster home of Lloyd and Gertrude.

I started kindergarten at St. Francis DeSalle Catholic School. My uniform was a white blouse with a plaid green/blue pleated jumper and tights with black and white saddle shoes. The nuns taught the classes in the basement of the church. Margaret and I always sat next to each other in the front. The church/school was on Humboldt Parkway located a few blocks from our home. We walked to school every day. I was the youngest, as well as the smallest, and everyone would leave me behind; so, I had to run to keep up with my brother and sisters. On Daisy Street, we passed a house where a big dog lived, and one day that dog got out and chased me to school because my foster siblings had left me behind. I became terrified to pass that house every day, so I made sure I ran faster to keep up.

We went home every day for lunch. I remember one winter afternoon, while we were sitting at the table eating grilled cheese and soup. Melvin sneezed, and it went into my bowl. I told Gertrude what he did, and she told me to eat it anyway. I could not believe she made me eat something that someone had sneezed into. I was about seven years old and knew it was nasty, so I took my time eating the grilled cheese until it was time to go back to school. I never finished the soup.

I attended St. Francis from Kindergarten through the first half of second grade.

It was early January 1969, when Lloyd and Gertrude moved the family out of Buffalo to a 23-acre farm in the country. I finished second grade at Farnham Elementary in Angola. It was a scary move because I did not know what to expect. I was used to being around Black people, and Farnham was all white. Students would always stare at us whenever we got on the bus. It was as if they had never seen Black people before.

People say that everyone remembers their third-grade teacher, and mine was Mrs. Christopher. She was an older white woman with gray hair. She turned out to be the nicest teacher in the entire Lake Shore School District. In June 1971, I was 10 years old when I graduated from the fourth grade at Farnham Elementary. By the time I reached fifth grade, the bullying and name-calling had already started.

As we grew older, the bus rides to school became more hostile. I realized the school system as well as the students were not used to being around Black people, even though there were a few other Blacks who attended the schools in the district. We were picked on and bullied just about every day of our school-age lives. We all had to take a yellow school bus and were some of the first students picked up by the driver. The white students would get on the bus and as they walked to the back to sit in their seats, they would call us niggers and sometimes hit us. Whenever we said something to the driver, he always said he didn't see anything.

I was in sixth grade when I realized how much I disliked being Black. Diane had braided my hair in cornrow braids and when I went to school the next day, the white students started laughing at me and calling me names. I hated it. I felt embarrassed and took the braids out, in the school bathroom. When I went back home, Gertrude asked me why I took them out, and when I explained my reasons, she started yelling at me saying, "Diane took her time to braid your hair and you took them out? You are so ungrateful!" At that point I did not care how they felt, it wasn't about them, it was about me feeling unwanted and not fitting in. For years, I disliked anything that represented Blackness because white people would only make fun of it and us.

I was twelve years old when I was forced to work in the fields in the hot sun and on rainy days. Gertrude took all my money like she did with my other siblings. We were given bologna or peanut butter and jelly sandwiches. I never liked the smell or taste of bologna.

In 1973/1974, bullying started to reach a point where we had no choice but to defend ourselves. We had to fight the racist students every day of our school-age years. We were called niggers, spit at, hit, pushed, and punched just because of the color of our skin. This went on day after day, year after year. Whenever Lloyd or Gertrude, mainly Gertrude, would go to the schools to talk about how we were being treated, the schools would either suspend us or put us in all-day or after-school detention. The white students never received discipline for their actions.

There was one specific family that caused all the trouble and hated Black people. The meanest of all was Jeffrey. One morning when he got on the bus – I believe I was in the seventh or eighth grade. He passed my brother, walked to my sister, Loretta, and stuck a pencil in her cheek. My brother and all the Black people started defending Loretta and fought back against him and his friends who jumped into the fight. I remember hiding on the floor between the seats to avoid getting hit. The driver pulled over and put all the Black students off the bus. That day the school superintendent and the high school principal called my parents to the school and informed them that he was suspending all of us for three days. He told Gertrude that we were not allowed to go anywhere. I believe that was on a Wednesday because I remember Gertrude had us pack clothes for a family trip. She felt if they were suspending us, she might as well take advantage of it.

I was looking forward to finally attending high school with my older siblings, but the excitement turned into disappointment when the district opened a new middle school in the fall of 1975. I had to wait another year. The bus rides were longer and became even more hostile. All Middle and High School students rode the same bus. My siblings and the other Black students stuck together to protect each other from the bullies. The fights never stopped. There was another big fight on the bus, this time with water guns. But it was not your typical water gunfight. The Black students had water mixed with ammonia, and the white students had water mixed with bleach. We were ducking and hiding between the seats while squirting our made-up concoctions at each other. The driver once again blamed the Black students. The detentions and suspensions increased, as well. Some of our teachers were just as racist as the students and they allowed the bullying to occur in their classrooms.

When I was finally able to attend high school with Loretta and Melvin, I thought I would be safe. That was not the case. I was always pushed and brushed up against throughout the day. There was a small platform looking over the first floor, and I remember a male student had threatened to throw me over the railing. I tried different ways to go to class, but nothing helped. My siblings were in a different area of the school and could not see what was happening to me. The more we told our parents, and the more they confronted the principal, the worse things became.

I was an honor student when the principal asked if I wanted to tutor elementary students in math and English. With all the turmoil he allowed to happen, I was surprised he had the audacity to even ask. Reluctantly I said yes. I took a school bus to their school once a week. In my third week of tutoring, one of the little boys said that his daddy told him not to listen to me. When I asked him why, he said he told his daddy I was Black. It was apparent his father did not want me teaching his son because of the color of my skin. I reported it to his teacher, and she honored the father's request.

At the end of tutoring, I returned to my school before the last period. The driver would drop me off at the door closest to the Senior study hall. The seniors watched me get off the bus. When I walked past their classroom door, they started with the name-calling and sometimes spitting at me. I was called Kizzy from the television miniseries "Roots," which started airing in January 1977. This went on week after week; and the teacher heard it, saw it, and ignored it.

When Melvin and Loretta graduated in 1977, many of the other Black students also graduated. I was basically by myself, except for one Black male.

I had to take biology and one day the teacher told the class that we would have to dissect a frog the following day. The teacher had the room set up with the frogs pinned to the little mat. One thing the teacher failed to mention was that we had to dissect the frog while it was still alive. He wanted us to see how the organs worked. There was no way I was going to cut open a frog. I was terrified and could not kill this ugly frog. I left the classroom with a few other female students. I failed that part of the class.

I always wanted to be an actress, so in my high school years, I started auditioning for the school chorus and musicals. I was a high soprano. The first musical I auditioned for was "The King and I." I did not get a part in either the chorus or the musical. The following year I auditioned for "Pippin" and was picked for the chorus as well as the opening dance number. I remember the Director giving the song, "Simple Joys" to a girl that really could not sing. She sang off-key, and I knew I could do better. I asked if I could at least sing it for him and he said no that he picked her for the song. I did my best to try and participate in the chorus and musicals, but I was held back because of my skin color. Our chorus director would repeatedly tell me that I was singing too loud and that I needed to lower my voice. He made me feel like I was not good enough to be a part of their productions. I began to feel intimidated by him and by the other students who would stare and kept telling me to sing lower. I carried this intimidation with me throughout my adulthood, which made me nervous to sing anything, and it showed.

I wanted to learn how to play an instrument. The school district allowed students to borrow any instrument for the year. Eventually, we had to buy our own. I started with the piccolo. Then, I switched to the flute for about six months. The next year, I tried the violin and saxophone. My favorite was the flute, but the family could not afford to buy me one. However, for my sixteenth birthday, Gertrude paid for me to take eight weeks of piano lessons.

I loved art and could paint and draw anything. I was in 10th grade when I painted a watercolor of a man who sailed around the world. I found the picture in "National Geographic." My art teacher loved it so much that he entered it in a contest at the Albright Knox Art Gallery in Buffalo. My painting was on display for several months. I discovered my own artistic ability at 5 years old, when I drew a picture of a dog on a washcloth Gertrude had given me. She thought I traced it and had me draw it again.

When I entered my Senior year in the fall of 1978, I was the only Black female in my class and had been since the eighth grade. I was still dealing with racism and bullying. Every day, for two hours after school, I started working a part-time job in the shipping and receiving department at the school. My female supervisor was nice, and we got along well. But there was one day when she had me opening packages and boxes to check to make sure the company sent the right items. There was a big white bucket that she told me had paint in it. But when I opened it, it was full of these huge cow eyes staring back at me. She laughed as I screamed as loud as I could. She thought it was funny that she scared me. She later explained that the eyes were needed for biology. I did not like her from that day forward and refused to open anything that came in buckets.

My senior year in high school was not glamorous at all. I worked at the school and had to give all my paychecks to Gertrude. I was not allowed to go to prom, and none of my siblings did either. Gertrude did not want to pay for them. The last musical I did was "Pippin," and the school tried its best to silence me. One of the most disappointing days in my life was when I was not able to graduate with my class. My racist English teacher failed me by one point and said that I needed to attend summer school to earn my diploma. I could not understand why, when I did every assignment and passed all my tests... yet he failed me. He waited until three days before graduation to tell me that I failed English.

I realized then how cruel and racist adults can be. He deliberately held me back. I was still being called names, not only by white people but by some of the Black people as well. There was one Black teenager who lived across the street with his grandmother; he used to call me banana, a wanna-be, Chiquita, Mulatto, yellow, half-white, and anything else he thought was offensive to me. I was glad when he moved to Buffalo.

I was supposed to be in the Debutante Ball and asked several times, but Gertrude did not want me to be a part of it. I just could not wait to get out of that house. I promised myself that I would go to the first college that accepted me that was the farthest away. So, I started applying to colleges that were at least two hundred miles or more from what was called home. My first acceptance letter came from the State University of New York at Oneonta, which is approximately 256 miles away, and I accepted it. I wanted to go to Juilliard for Acting, but no one could afford it. Since I was a foster child, I was able to go to college for free if it was a state college, so Juilliard was not an option. But I was happy that somebody wanted me!

In the summer of 1979, I attended summer school in June for a few hours and worked as a camp counselor at Evangola State Park for the Town of Evans. For the first time, I was able to keep some of my money. I was happily preparing for my escape to college. It was mid-August and time to get the heck out of Dodge. Lloyd and Gertrude decided they would take me to Oneonta in the family motor home. So, the few foster children, including two new ones, all went with us. We left early in the morning and drove five hours to Oneonta. It was a fun drive for me. When we arrived, I thought it was strange that Lloyd stayed in the motor home, while Gertrude and my other siblings helped to take my things to the dorm. The saddest thing about it all was no one helped me set up my room. They all got back into the motor home, said bye, and pulled off. Not a hug, not a congratulations, not we're proud of you, nothing but bye. I was in shock as I watched them drive out of sight. I stood there for a few minutes in tears as I watched other parents and students hugging each other.

When I walked back to my room, I stood there for a few minutes, still with tears, watching parents as they helped their children set up their rooms. My roommate came in with her parents, as well. At that moment, I really wanted my parents to show love towards me and my accomplishments. I knew I was more than a state check.

Later that night, while sitting in my dorm room, I wrote a 23-page letter to Lloyd and Gertrude regarding Margaret and how they treated her. I wanted them to know, whether they cared or not, how sending her away affected me. I felt they needed to know my pain. Gertrude never said anything to me about it. She did tell me about fifteen years ago that she still had that letter.

My first year of college was a lot of fun, filled with new beginnings, new lessons, new friends, and new ideas. It was almost a culture shock for me because I had never been to a school with so many Black people. Oneonta was about 150 miles from New York City and was filled with students from the five boroughs. I began to realize how sheltered I was, growing up. I never knew anything about marijuana or joints, as they called it in school. The students smoked it all the time and offered it to me. I said no every time. It had a nasty smell and people would pass the same joint from person to person. That was nasty to me and very un-ladylike. Drinking became another issue at parties. I remembered the awful time when our grandmother tried to give us beer, so I refused to drink alcohol, as well. My peers often called me a square because I refused to participate in what I considered detrimental to my health and well-being. I did start drinking wine coolers, but it would take me a few days to drink one.

I soon learned how divided and racist Oneonta was. It reminded me of Lake Shore. They had a cheerleading squad, which was all white, and a rhythm squad, which was all Black. I made the rhythm in my first year. We participated in all the basketball and soccer games, but our uniforms were old and worn out, unlike those of the "white" cheerleaders. The drama department was divided in such a way that Black people had their own productions and whites had theirs. The Black productions were held annually while the white productions were held twice a year and were heavily funded. Dr. Ernest Battle was a Black Theater Professor who taught certain classes. He was also the Director of the annual productions. He was a father figure to many of the Black students. I was in all his classes until he was murdered in 1982. He would always tell me, "Never give up, you're going to be a star one day."

My first college production was a play titled "Freeman". I played the character Osa Lee who had a southern accent. I was overjoyed when Dr. Battle told me I had the part. I felt I was on my way to becoming a known actress. In that production, the script called for my husband, the main character, to slap me in the face. Dr. Battle demonstrated to both of us how to fake slap someone, which we rehearsed several times. But the guy told me he was going to really slap me on one of the three nights. I thought he was joking. But on the second night, when Gertrude and Diane came from Buffalo to see me perform, he really slapped me hard. I remember standing there in disbelief, but I had to deliver my lines before I stormed off stage. He slapped me so hard that I bit the inside of my mouth and was bleeding. I remember walking off that stage in disbelief and slamming the door so hard, that a picture fell off the set wall. I was so mad at him and told the crew I was not going back out there. Needless to say, I did finish the show and slapped him back afterward. Dr. Battle knew what he did, but said it was a great performance.

When my first year at Oneonta ended, I returned home as an honor student. I remember Gertrude opening my report card that was addressed to me. She seemed a little proud of me when she said that I had made the Dean's list with all A's.

After I completed my first year in college, I bought my first car with leftover grant money. It was an orange Ford Mustang with white leather seats and a white racing stripe down the middle. I bought it from the Seneca Nation Reservation for $100. The car had a lot of grass and weeds growing inside of it. I was able to clean it out and make a few repairs. I drove that car all summer long. I remember the first time I ran out of gas and had to coast it down a hill into the gas station. I didn't think it was going to make it! The car only lasted for that summer. The steering column broke one day while I was in Buffalo. I called Lloyd, who was a self-made mechanic, to see if he could come and get it for me; but for some reason, he said he didn't have time. So, I called another family friend who lived only a few blocks away. He was able to remove it from the street the next day. Unfortunately for me, I was leaving to go back to college the following day and was not able to get it fixed. Gertrude was very angry with me that I called on someone else, and she accused me of having sex with this much older family friend. He was a father figure, and his daughter and I were like sisters. We met at a young age and remained friends for years. I used to travel places with him, his wife, and his daughter. Gertrude, just out of the blue said, "You must be screwing him." I thought, *how sick and disgusting can she be?* I later found out that he was someone she used to date before she met Lloyd.

I went home during the usual college breaks and for a few weekends throughout the semesters. Whenever I called Gertrude to let her know, she would always ask who was coming, Judy or Mary. She felt I had dual personalities because I am a Gemini. She never liked the way I stood up for myself, the more mature I became. I would jokingly say, Judy. But said to myself, *it depends on whether you make me angry.* I knew she always tried to provoke me and would purposely try to upset me.

My second and third years at Oneonta taught me a lot about life. I decided to move off campus and rent a house with friends. I was the Secretary for the Black Student Union for both years. I still sang in the gospel choir, and instead of trying for the all-Black Rhythm Squad, I decided to try out for the all-white Cheerleaders. I felt they needed to be a little diversified. I had to learn their routine, which included flips, cartwheels, and splits. So, for several weeks, I practiced and on the day of the tryouts, I was still having a little difficulty doing a full split. I was determined to make the squad, so I started my routine, then I faked a sprained ankle and explained to the judges how I was unable to complete the split because of it. The next day when I checked the list, my name was on it as an alternate. I was also interested in Sorority life, so I decided to pledge Sigma Gama Phi, Arethusa. It too was all white. There were no Black sororities or fraternities in Oneonta. Pledging was wild and crazy. All the girls drank, but me. I was not about to do what they were all doing, and I still managed to cross over.

I wanted to learn how to swim, ever since my first near-drowning incident. A group of my friends said they could teach me. So, we went for a late-night swim at the college pool. One of them told me the easiest way to learn is to jump off the diving board into the deep end. They all cleared the pool and watched as I dove in. I made it back up and to the side of the pool. Everyone was clapping and cheering me on. I couldn't believe I did it. I was just as excited and tried it again ten minutes later. No one was watching me this time. I dove in, turned my body around, and thought I had made it to the top. When I opened my eyes and mouth, I started choking from the water. I had not made it to the top. The next thing I remember was someone pulling me out of the water.

On weekends my friends and I would often dance and party at the "Dark Horse." It was also the place to meet new people from the surrounding colleges. I was in my 3rd year when a young Caucasian guy approached me at the club. He introduced himself and said he had been watching me for several weeks. At that moment I became a little nervous, but I was surrounded by friends just in case he tried anything. He told me everything he knew about me including my name, where I was from, and what I was majoring in. He then asked if I had ever done any modeling before. I thought about the fashion shows we did for Gertrude a few times and said, "Yes I did." He then said he was an editor for a major magazine and thought I would be perfect for their next issue. I was still looking at him with skepticism and had no idea what he was talking about. I finally stopped him and asked, "What magazine?" He said, "Playboy." I knew he could tell by the expression on my face that I was getting upset with him. He quickly said, "You don't have to take any clothes off. You will be with a few other females, and we will pay you $100,000. When I said no, he gave me his card and told me to think about it. The next day, I called Gertrude and told her about my encounter. I was surprised when she said, "That would be a big mistake if you did it."

I auditioned for all the plays and received leading roles. My favorite was Beneatha in "A Raisin in The Sun." It was the last production Professor Battle directed before his murder. I had just seen him the day before when I handed in an assignment. His murder was a complete shock to the entire Black Student body. None of us knew what to do. We were trying to figure out how to continue without him. The white professors who took over his classes for the remaining semester replaced the "A" I had received with a "C." The theater department did not like the fact that I was interviewed by news reporters who wrote an article regarding Professor Battle's death.

My Senior year at Oneonta was difficult. The only Black Drama Professor was murdered the previous semester which made it hard to concentrate. I knew the other theater professors were upset with the Black student body and getting an "A" in their classes was impossible.

I met a lot of nice guys and dated two while attending Oneonta. I got pregnant and was put under a lot of stress by the baby's father. He wanted me to get an abortion, but I refused. He made my life a living hell to the point I was stressing out and failing my classes. I felt I had no choice but to quit and go home. When I told Gertrude about the ordeal, she knew it before I could finish telling her. She and Lloyd were so angry with me for quitting school. But I had to do what I felt was best for me. He said I had my hand on the doorknob and failed. I went home in April 1983 and gave birth to my son, Jeffrey, on July 20th. I knew I did not want to continue living with them and they definitely did not want me there either. They looked at me as a failure. So, I joined the Army in October 1983 and left for boot camp on January 19, 1984.

5

Recalling the Numerous Residences of My Childhood

I was eight months old when I arrived at Lloyd and Gertrude Colbert's home on a snowy February morning. This was Lloyd and Gertrude Colbert's first home. It was a yellow two-story, three-bedroom/1 bath house with a pink basement. There was a two-car garage behind the house with a small yard for us to play in.

17 Viola Park

The house had a large porch with hedges in the front and on the right-side walkway, leading to the stairs. I remember how I used to play with the roly-poly (potato) bugs that would curl up when I touched them. We would often sit on the porch but were not allowed to leave it.

The front door opened into a large living room, which led to the dining room and into the kitchen. The boys' bedroom was a small room off from the kitchen. The stairs to the basement were near the back door, which also led to the driveway, garage, and play area.

The stairs to the second floor were in the dining room. There was a long hallway at the top of the stairs, which led into the bedrooms and bathroom. Lloyd and Gertrude's room was to the left and the girls' room was to the right. There was a railing where we were able to look down over the stairs and see parts of the dining room, as well as the kitchen.

All the neighbors on the block watched out for each other. Gertrude would always visit with the Browns, who lived two doors to the left. As we grew older, we were able to leave the porch and play with the neighborhood children in the grassy median.

We would often play hide-n-seek, dodgeball, and kickball; but we had to be in the house before the streetlights came on.

I was six years old when Gertrude sent me to my room to get something she needed. It was completely dark. I pulled down on the ceiling light string that was in the middle of our room and when it came on, there was a huge rubber black widow spider dangling in my face. I remember screaming and crying, as I ran downstairs. She laughed when she heard and saw how terrified I was. Gertrude had tied it on the string to purposely scare me. She always threw that spider at Margaret and me to chase us out of the crawl space in our bedroom. I started having nightmares of creepy things crawling all over my bed and would wake up in the middle of the night, screaming.

I remember the Harley Davidson motorcycles that Lloyd and Gertrude owned in the early 1970s. Lloyd started The Buffalo Trojans as well as the Buffalo Monarchs Motorcycle Clubs. Gertrude was a member of a nationwide all-female club called The Cycle Queens of America. One morning when our grandmother was watching us, they rode their motorcycles to an event with other club members. A few hours later, Lloyd came home and told us Gertrude was in an accident and had to be taken to the hospital. He said that one of their friends accidentally drove his motorcycle into the back of Gertrude's causing her to fall. The accident caused a small burn mark on her face and injured both legs. I remember all of us crying and asking him if she was going to die. She stayed overnight and came home the next day on crutches. That burn mark remains on her face.

As we grew older, neighborhood gangs began to pop up and take over the streets. There was an incident at the neighborhood Boys Club. Melvin won a trophy from a pool tournament but was threatened by a few older boys. The Club called Gertrude because he was too scared to walk home by himself. She sent Loretta and Diane to walk back with him. Shortly afterward, our family left Buffalo and moved thirty miles out to the countryside. Gertrude rented the Viola Park house to a friend and her five children. *Lloyd and Gertrude later gave the house to Melvin. It was then given to his ex-wife during their divorce settlement. Gertrude and Lloyd were extremely angry with him for letting the house go.*

363 Maiden Lane Road

Lloyd and Gertrude bought a farmhouse, which was located on twenty-three acres of land, from Mr. Walker who was a good friend of theirs. He also owned a funeral home in Buffalo and did not want the country property to sit vacant. I remember overhearing a conversation between Gertrude and their attorney years later, stating that he sold it to them for just one dollar. The farmland was in Farnham about thirty miles from Buffalo off Route 5.

We moved there during our Spring break in March 1969. I was seven years old and still in the second grade. This place holds so many good, bad, and ugly memories.

Maiden Lane is about a mile-long dead-end road, which the town of Brant paved with white gravel each spring. Three other families lived at the end. Cows were grazing in the green grass behind a barbed wire fence on the right side of the road. Once you passed the grazing cows, you would see multiple rows of growing corn stalks and grapevines with purple grapes. Lloyd and Gertrude purchased all the land on the left side. There were tall trees that aligned the road and the open field. A quarter of the way down was a long driveway that led to a two-story farmhouse with a garage and a one-bedroom tiny brick house. The address was 345 Maiden Lane. A little bridge in the road covered the water that flowed from the pond.

The little brick house at 345

The 363 Maiden Lane farmhouse was halfway up the road. It had a U-shaped driveway that circled the grass with a medium-sized cherry tree growing in the middle. Next to the tree was an old, rusted well with a pump. The main two-story house was built with the right side facing the road. There was a two-level barn on the right side. Behind the house was a wide pond with a wobbly metal plank bridge. A smaller two-story house with an attached garage stood directly across from the main house.

The main house had a porch that wrapped around to the right, with a wooden railing. Small bushes aligned the front. There were three entrances. The main entrance opened into the family room that was originally the kitchen. Upon entering the den, there was a set of stairs on the left leading to the upstairs bedrooms. Under those stairs was a small closet that Gertrude used as a pantry and storage for her cooking items. Next to the closet was the furnace heater that warmed half of the house. In the winter we had to put a pot of water on it every few hours to help keep the house humid. The bathroom was just to the right. The family room led into the dining room. The kitchen was to the right with a wide ledge to serve food in the dining room. The kitchen had a pantry that Lloyd added to hold the rest of Gertrude's cooking and catering supplies. He also added another door that led to the backyard and pond.

The dining and living rooms were adjacent to each other. The living room had a furnace that sat against the left wall which kept the other half of the house warm. Next to the furnace was the second entrance, which was seldom used. Diane's piano sat against the side wall, facing inward. The right side of the living room had a doorway, with a coat closet and another set of stairs that led to the bedrooms. Against that wall was a couch, where Lloyd always sat in the dark watching the fish swim around in the large tank. He would often scare me when I came down the stairs because I never noticed him until he moved or said something.

There were two ways to get to the bedrooms. You could walk up the stairs in the family room or use the stairs in the living room hallway. We often chased each other, running through the house by going up one way and coming down the other. The living room stairs were mainly used to enter the girls' side. Loretta, Margaret, and I shared a room, so our room was first. Margaret and I had bunk beds and Loretta had her own. The upstairs furnace was in our room. Diane's private room was to the right of ours. We were not allowed to enter her room. There were nights when we lay on the floor next to her door and talked for hours. Whenever we got hungry in the middle of the night, we took turns sneaking downstairs to get toothpaste. We would put it on our fingers, go back to our room, and share it with each other. We were never caught.

I never considered our bedroom to be a safe haven for any of us. It was difficult to sleep because we never knew when Gertrude was going to wake any of us up by beating us with switches, the motorcycle belt, or the ironing cord. I would hear her coming up the stairs and would try hiding under the cover to protect myself. She would snatch it off and beat us anyway. It did not matter to her where she was hitting us. We had marks and bruises all over our bodies.

We tried running away from her to avoid the beatings. Gertrude then started locking us in the bathroom and she made us take off our clothes. She beat us butt naked, so we could not run out. She started hitting us with the switches, ironing cord, or Lloyd's motorcycle belt while we were getting undressed. It was like she couldn't wait to start torturing us and would never get tired. It seemed the more she hit us, the stronger her demeanor became. The switches, belts, and ironing cords left bruises and bloody marks on our little bodies. I remember so many times when she made me sit in a tub of cold water to limit the swelling. I sat in that tub and watched the water turn pink from my bleeding body.

On the left side of our room was the doorway that led into the boys' room. Their room led to the small hallway and stairs. Directly across was the doorway which led into Lloyd and Gertrude's room. It was the largest of the three with bigger windows that peered out to the front and left side of the house.

There was no running water when we first moved in. We had to go outside with buckets and pots to pump water from the well, even in the night hours. It smelled like rotten eggs and tasted bitter from the sulfur.

The yard was huge and pitch black at night. The only streetlight was near the small bridge. Lloyd eventually had a light installed in the center of the yard. The grass was noticeably tall and thick. In the spring we were given grass sickles and slingers to chop it down. Lloyd finally bought a tractor with a grass cutter and a plow to cut the larger fields and the garden. Gertrude would have us pick the dandelions that covered the yard for her homemade dandelion wine. *That was some of the nastiest stuff.*

There were snakes everywhere and I was terrified of them. They would wrap themselves around the small bushes in front of the house and hide in the cracks of the concrete stairs leading to the porch. I remember sitting with a shovel waiting for them to peek their heads out so I could try to kill them with it. We always had to be careful, walking around in the spring and summer months. I remember one day when we were returning from the grocery store, Lloyd and my brothers were standing on the sidewalk next to the driveway. They were looking down at something that looked big and black to me. Gertrude then said, Lloyd must have killed a snake, and it was bigger than usual. I remember sitting in our maroon and white van waiting to take the groceries into the house. I knew I did not want to go near any of that. So, I sat there waiting for them to pick it up and move it out of the way. Gertrude told me to take the food into the house. I grabbed a bag, stepped out of the van, and tried to maneuver my way through the yard. My brother Corey picked up the bloody dead snake with a pitchfork and ran after me with it. All I wanted to do was get away from him. I was halfway to the house when I dropped the groceries and ran back to the van. As I stepped up to get in, my foot slipped. I fell backward and hit the ground. When I looked up, Corey was standing over me holding that bloody snake. I was terrified.

The entire house needed a serious paint job, inside and out. There were field mice that moved in before we did. Lloyd used to set traps and we could hear them snap in the middle of the night. Missy and Sissy were two black and white cats that they bought to help get rid of the mice. One evening after returning home, Gertrude noticed that they had jumped on the counter and eaten some of the grease she left out. She got angry and threw them outside in the dark. We never saw them again.

The house was like a summer camp during the first few years. Lloyd and Gertrude's friends would send their children to stay with us throughout the summer. They felt it was safe and it gave them an opportunity to see what living in the country was like. We were treated better whenever there were other children around. Gertrude would take all of us to the Drive-In movies in Angola. The first movie we saw was "Ben." It was my all-time favorite. I now realize she did it to make a good impression on her friends. Once everyone left and stopped coming for the summer, all hell broke loose, and Gertrude's slave mentality set back in.

There was a variety of wild animals. We would often wake up in the morning and see deer grazing in the yard and drinking water out of the pond. That pond had all types of creepy things that swam with the fish. As soon as the sun set, the frogs would start to croak all through the night.

Bats flew around the lights. They chased us every time we walked down the road going to our grandmother's house. We had to duck and run as fast as we could, so they would not swoop down over our heads.

We had a mid-size brown pony named Bell that slept in the barn and ate the grass in the backyard that led to the pond. She would often escape across it and eat the apples off the trees at our grandmother's house. All the other children that came for the summer wanted to ride her. Loretta was the only one who could ride without falling off. She was able to sit on her backwards and lay on her back without Bell bucking her off. I remember my younger brothers and I had to use a bucket to mount her. We never had a saddle, so we held on to her long mane. I remember a time when I climbed on her, and she took off running down the hill towards the pond. I was holding on as tight as I could, but I was bouncing up and down and fell off right at the pond. She kept running and her hoof grazed my shoulder. I lay on the ground crying for help, but no one could hear me. I gradually picked myself up and went into the house. I did not try riding her anymore, after that incident. It was as if she knew I was a little intimidated. However, I would still try to groom her, which she seemed to like.

The barn was also a shelter for all the dogs we had. It seemed like new dogs were showing up every month. There was Gunsmoke, a big mixed-breed fluffy dog. Chico was a beige Cocker Spaniel that ran into the house and hid under the TV during thunderstorms. Jason was a black and white Beagle that protected us at any cost. One day, he was attacked by a neighbor's

German Shepard named Ren Tin Tin. He broke his chain, like he always did, ran across Route 5, through the fields, grabbed Jason by the neck, and started swinging him around. We managed to break up the fight, but Jason sustained a severe neck injury. Lloyd wanted to shoot him because he felt Jason was suffering; so, I hid him in the barn and took care of him. Jason healed himself by rubbing his neck on the green grass until the hole closed by itself. Everybody was shocked that he survived.

Red was a big red Irish Setter that we all loved and played with. He tried to chase the school bus one morning and accidentally hanged himself with the chain he was tied to on the upper level of the barn. I remember all of us were crying when Gertrude was explaining the tragic accident. Another dog that just appeared on the farm was a little fluffy mixed dog that Gertrude named Hobo. There was also a dog named Patches who looked like he had different color patches made for a coat. Chico was a Chihuahua that was able to stay in the house. Sheila was a German Shepard mixed breed that stayed with us for a while. Many of the dogs would disappear back into the fields, never to be seen again. I do remember a time when one of the dogs had puppies and Gertrude did not want them around. So, she put them in a box and dropped them in an open field near the Reservation. I started crying as we drove away because I knew they were not going to survive being away from their mother.

Gertrude's mother, Esther (Grandma), and her husband, Abram (Granddaddy), moved to the country with us. They lived at 345, which was the first two-story house on the road.

345 Maiden Lane

There was a long driveway that led to the garage. In the middle of the driveway was a small 1-bedroom brick house. Lloyd's grandmother, Flora, also lived there for a brief time; but she decided she did not like the country and went back to Buffalo. Different apple trees were aligned on one side of the house. My favorites were the golden apples. A two-acre open field and our garden were on the other side of the trees. We planted all kinds of fruits and vegetables, but my favorite was the tomatoes. I would pick one, wash it, and sprinkle it with a little salt while eating it. I enjoyed working in the garden until I saw a snake, and I did not want to go out there anymore. Grandma said, "It's just a harmless garden snake, it can't hurt you." I didn't care what type it was. To me, a snake is a snake.

There was a huge lilac bush on the side of Grandma's house, near the back porch that blossomed every spring with purple and white lilacs. We had to be careful not to get stung by the bees that surrounded it. The flowers smelled so good, as well as added freshness and color to her backyard. Margaret and I would break off a few branches and put them in cups.

Esther worked at Norbans, a high-end clothing store in Buffalo. She would buy all of us new clothes every Easter. I was around nine years old when she bought the girls new dresses with matching coats. While I was trying the dress on, my coat accidentally slid off the chair and hit the floor. Gertrude saw the coat on the floor and began yelling, saying, "You are so ungrateful, and you don't deserve anything." When I tried to explain that the coat slid off the chair, she began hitting me and would not allow me to defend myself over the accident.

Esther was also a hairdresser. Lloyd redesigned her back room into a hair salon. There was the big black sink and the big hair dryer that we sat under. She always burned our scalp in several places when she used the hot comb to flatten our hair before putting it in pigtails. Many of her friends drove out to the country so she could do their hair.

Esther loved to entertain and host parties. I was around twelve years old when I slipped on ice outside her home one winter evening and cut my knee. I was carrying a roasting pan filled with fried chicken that Diane had just prepared. Margaret and I were walking on the side of the house when I slipped and fell in the snow. I was trying to hold the pan so none of the chicken would fall out. I knew they were waiting for it and I did not want to get in trouble, so I was happy that none of it landed on the ground. When Margaret and I walked in, I told Gertrude and the other guests what had just happened. I then said, "I think my knee is bleeding." When I pulled down my snow pants, we saw blood everywhere. Apparently, glass from a broken window was mixed in the snow where I fell. Gertrude and Granddaddy tried washing my knee, but it would not stop bleeding. They took me to the hospital, where I had to get five stitches. It was very painful when that Doctor stuck the needle in the cut to numb it. I still have the scar.

Esther was a member of the Order of the Eastern Star, Buffalo Chapter. I never understood what they did, other than have Tea Celebrations where everyone dressed up in white with fancy hats and matching white gloves. They attended all the Masonic Lodge events that Lloyd was a member of, as well. One year, Gertrude had an idea to have us children start a singing group that would perform at Grandma's Tea. I was around nine or ten years old. We were happy to get new clothes when Gertrude bought us bell bottoms, matching shirts, and white Converse all-star sneakers. We rehearsed "ABC" and "Signed, Sealed, Delivered" for the show. Corey was the youngest, so she picked him as the lead singer. She said people would like him better and throw more money on the stage. We did sing "ABC," even though Corey could not sing or remember some of the words. I felt he ruined it for the rest of us because we were not allowed to sing the second song. We were told there was not enough time for another song. Gertrude took the only $5 bill that a lady had put on the stage. That was our first and last performance.

Esther loved to smoke Camel cigarettes and drink Heineken beer and Crown Royal whiskey. She always had a purple Crown Royal bag whenever she came over. Holiday parties, birthday parties, and any celebrations at our house would always end with her storming out inebriated and mad. She and Uncle George (Grandma Flora's husband) would get very inebriated and argue. He always cracked jokes that offended her to the point where she would get up, cuss him out, and slam the door as she walked out. I would always laugh to myself and eventually go upstairs to my room. My sisters and I would say, here they go again. He called all of us winos.

Abram wanted to raise chickens and decided to turn one of the smaller shacks into a chicken coup. The roosters and chickens were always near the pond. Every time any of us tried to cross it, the two roosters would chase us and peck our legs. I learned to use a stick to keep them away from me. I had to go to their coup to collect the eggs that Gertrude used. It was smelly, nasty, and full of chicken poop. One thing I hated the most was watching them die. My grandfather would grab a chicken by its neck and swing it around until it snapped. The chicken would run around flapping its wings for several minutes before it died. Or he would chop its head off with an axe, watch it run around, flapping its wings, until it died. Gertrude would then put the dead chicken in a big pot of boiling water for several minutes. She had us sit on the family room floor and pluck the feathers off the dead chicken. The horrific smell made me nauseated. Even though I was forced to sit at the table until my plate was empty, I never ate any of the chickens that I watched them kill. *I was grateful we had dogs in the house.*

Cleaning chitlins was another smelly task the girls had to do. Gertrude would buy these red buckets, full of nasty chitlins during the winter holidays. My sisters and I had to clean the smelly intestines by pulling the crap off them. Gertrude gave them a second cleaning, then put them in a big pot to cook for hours. When they finished boiling, she would sit the pot outside in the snow to cool overnight. The house smelled like pure doo-doo. I tasted them once and said, "Never again!" I was happy when she said they were for the guests.

Gertrude often bought pig feet, deer and rabbit meat, and a few other things from the nearby Reservation. I was sitting at the dinner table one Sunday and asked Gertrude for more beef. She said it's not beef, it's venison. I asked, "What is that?" She said, "Deer meat." At that moment I became nauseated and could not eat anything else. I was so angry that she did not give us a choice, whether or not to eat Bambi. All I could do was envision the deer we often saw in our yard peacefully grazing in the grass. There was another Sunday dinner when I bit down on a small hard object. When I showed it to her, she said it was a pellet. I said, "A pellet in the chicken?" She replied, "You're eating rabbit." I looked at my plate and could only envision a furry bunny. I could not believe that she would feed us anything and lie about it.

Granddaddy Abram died from a heart attack in 1977. He went fishing and was walking up a hill to his car. Another fisherman found his body.

I was ten years old when Gertrude and Lloyd started the motorcycle field meets. Lloyd cleared about three acres of bushes and grass with the tractor and plow. The straight racetrack was about 150 yards long. Bushes, tall grass, and trees aligned the left side of the track. The spectator's area was aligned with rolls of used tires to prevent any injuries from out-of-control racers. The spectators and competitors parked their vehicles, set up lawn chairs, tables, and grills, and enjoyed the races. An old milk truck was fixed up and used as the concession stand where Gertrude sold hot dogs, hamburgers, corn on the cob, pop, and different chips for $1. I always worked at the entrance gate with Grandmother Esther, collecting money from the attendees. The races were held just about every Sunday during the summer months. In July, The Cycle Queens of America held their annual race. It was called "The Big One," because people from all over the U.S. traveled by motorcycles, campers, and trailers hitched to cars to camp out on the track grounds for the weekend. A motorcade and party were held on the Saturday before the races. The club's colors were red and white. It was amazing to see so many women dressed in white pants with matching boots, and their red motorcycle jackets.

Lloyd was the founder of the Buffalo Monarchs and The Empire State Trojans Motorcycle Clubs. He later started a coed youth team for our family and friends called the Grape Belt Strokers Motorcycle and Competition Team. The jacket's logo was a bundle of grapes with the team's name. The girls were only used for the game portion. I was around twelve years old when I first started going to the track with Lloyd and my siblings, so he could teach us to ride. Thank goodness for the tires that aligned the track.

We often traveled to Rochester for the Rochester Road Knights races. The owners were Lloyd and Gertrude's best friends, so their track meets were very similar to ours. Other places we traveled to for races were Kentucky, Indiana, and Ohio. There was a young all-male racing team in Cleveland, called Family Beverages. They were my favorite team and I always looked forward to seeing them at the events. I had a serious crush on one of them. His name was Dwayne. I always made sure that he was my partner wherever we went. He had a yellow 125 Suzuki and I felt he could out-race anybody. I will never forget the time when we entered the boot race at one of my family's competitions. His motorcycle was facing towards the finish line. I had one hand on the back seat and was facing in the opposite direction. When the referee blew his whistle, I ran down to the pile of boots, put mine on, and ran back towards the motorcycle. When I put my hands on the back seat to jump on, Dwayne took off as fast as he could, and I landed in the dirt; not to mention in front of all the people who were staring at me. I was so embarrassed. His father started laughing as he helped me off the ground. Dwayne made it to the finish line without me. He came back apologizing, saying he thought I was on his bike. We are still friends!

Evangola State Park was only a half-mile from where we lived. Gertrude would often send us to the beach to collect seashells and pieces of driftwood for the yard. I wanted to learn how to swim and decided to teach myself. I knew my brother was watching me as I walked into the lake. All of a sudden, I was unable to feel the ground under my feet and the water was starting to cover my face. I could see the water right under my nose. I was yelling for help and trying not to panic. My brother who was unable to swim was screaming, "Walk backwards!" A few seconds later I was able to feel the ground under my feet again and made my way back to shore. I thought I was going to drown. I never did that again… after that day, I only allowed the water to cover my ankles.

363 Maiden Lane Road was also the start of many new things. Lloyd joined the Masons and became a Shriner of Hadji Temple #61. The temple had a marching band that Gertrude allowed us to join. Margaret and I were majorettes, Loretta was a flag girl and Diane carried the American flag. I liked wearing my short majorette uniform with white boots and a tassel that moved back and forth every time we marched and danced to the music.

Shortly after moving to Farnham, Lloyd and Gertrude bought a Coachman motorhome. I will never forget one family trip we took to Florida to visit Gertrude's long-lost sister. I was 11 years old. On the day we arrived, her neighbor decided to use a roach bomb. I watched those bugs as they came out from under the door, the windows, and on the ground. This was all new to me because I had never seen a roach before. They were all sizes and some of them had wings. It was so creepy to me but did not seem to bother any of the adults. That night we had to sleep in her apartment and the bugs were crawling everywhere. I asked if I could sleep in the motorhome. Gertrude said, no the adults were sleeping there. I was too scared to fall asleep.

My brothers went to the nearby park to play basketball with some of the boys in the neighborhood. Margaret, Loretta, and I were walking to join them when a group of girls confronted us. They started calling us names and said we did not belong there. My brothers came to our rescue by telling them we were their sisters. They said we were too light to be their sisters. This was a rude awakening for us to know that some Black people did not like us because we were not black enough. A few of them wanted to be our friends only because they liked our brothers.

We stayed with Gertrude's sister for a week. I was so happy when it was time to leave. The return trip was just as adventurous. Lloyd had just turned onto the Florida turnpike when somebody saw a roach. It disappeared down one of the back seats. Lloyd quickly pulled over. We had to shake all our clothes outside. Gertrude took all the food and dishes out of the cabinets to see if any more bugs somehow got into the trailer. Lloyd found the stowaway hiding under the seat and threw it outside after he killed it.

He continued driving for a few more hours, and then someone said they were thirsty. All the water, juice, and pop were already devoured. There was only Grandma's Heineken left in the refrigerator. She poured each of us a small amount. I took a sip and started gagging from the nasty bitter taste. Margaret drank hers and the rest of mine without any problem. I do believe that was the start and main cause of her drinking habit. I was surprised that we were given beer to drink at such an early age.

The Blizzard of '77 was the worst winter storm that ever hit the Western New York area. It was said to be a 200-year weather event. It all started on the evening of January 27, 1977. It was snowing and the wind was gusting over 60 mph. Snowpacks were over thirty inches in some areas. I could hear the wind blowing through the doors and windows of the house. The snow drifts were so high we were not able to go outside. Our schools were always the last to close, but that blizzard closed them for several days. People were using snowmobiles and skis to get around. The trees, ground, and roads were covered with snow and ice. We were stuck in the house, unable to go anywhere for days. When we were finally able to go outside and play in the snow, we built lots of snowmen and made igloos with the high snowdrifts. Lloyd worked a lot of overtime plowing the streets and would stay with family members during the week.

As the years passed by, many different things went on with the 363 Maiden Lane Road property. In the mid-'70s Lloyd and Gertrude started having problems with the Walker family. Mr. Walker had a daughter, Dorothy, who felt the property should have been given to her. After he died in a tragic fire, she contacted an attorney to open an investigation into the sale of 363. They discovered that Lloyd and Gertrude had not paid taxes on the property in years. Dorothy and her attorney fought to regain what she considered to be her family's property. There were many phone calls that Gertrude refused to answer. She would tell us to answer the phone and say they were not there. This went on for several years. I know I didn't mind telling the callers she wasn't there.

Gertrude made it seem like our family was being targeted by Dorothy. When my siblings and I were left alone at home, we started making prank phone calls to the Walker Funeral Home. We also ordered boxes of pizzas and had them delivered to the funeral home. We knew our calls could not be tracked if we hit star 67 before we dialed. However, there was one time when we did not dial it first. We received a call back from the restaurant saying they could not deliver the pizza. They knew we pranked them, and we were scared that they would call the police, so we turned off the lights and sat in the dark until Lloyd and Gertrude returned home. We never pranked the funeral home or pizza parlor again.

St. John Baptist Church located in Buffalo, became our family church home. I was around twelve years old when we first started attending. Gertrude joined the mass choir and became one of their lead singers. She loved the attention; I believe she joined for the notoriety that she gained. My sisters and I joined the Youth Choir. I was a high soprano. Margaret and Loretta were altos. We traveled each year for Youth Choir conventions. Diane and our brothers never joined the choir. The church is where I met two other fine young men. One broke my heart after I saw him with another girl at a house party. I drew a portrait of him and handed it to his mother one Sunday, letting her know I did not want to see her son anymore. I dated my other friend for a year but ended the relationship when we started college. I visited St. John when my sons were much younger and was happy to show them pictures of me and the choir displayed on the second-floor walls.

363 was the start of many friendships. Some were short, but there were a few that lasted through the years. The first neighbor I met was a six-year-old girl named Desiree. We met on the school bus. She lived with her parents on Route 5, just across Maiden Lane. Our families met soon afterward, and we became good friends. She joined our motorcycle team, went to church with us, and participated in just about everything we did. She was seventeen when she moved to Buffalo with her mother. Margaret and I would often go to her house to play music, and call boys. In the summer months, we covered our bodies with butter and laid on her blacktop driveway hoping to get a deep tan. Growing up, I considered Desiree to be my best friend and would tell people we were cousins. Through the years, we stayed in contact

with each other off and on. I learned that sometimes you outgrow old friends, when you realize that all you have in common is your past.

10880 Erie Road

I was in middle school when Lloyd and Gertrude managed to purchase the 12-acre property we called "the house on 5." It was a three-story house that needed repairs. It had a basement, first floor, and an attic that was used as a bedroom. The basement had two entrances, which I thought was a little unusual. The family room had a door built into the floor. The outside entrance had a door that was built into the ground, like a tornado hideaway.

Both properties were now connected. The entrance to the motorcycle races was changed to the added property after Lloyd cleared a path and built a dirt road, which led to the open field and track.

Lloyd was always remodeling the houses we lived in. One day I tripped over a piece of wood with a rusty nail sticking out of it. The nail pierced the side of my knee and was sticking out. Gertrude removed the nail and my knee started bleeding, even more. I was only twelve, but I knew I needed to go to the hospital. Instead, she poured bleach over the hole. I screamed from the pain, not only from the nail but also from the bleach. It took a while for my knee to heal.

My younger brother Corey always used to bother me. One day while in the house, I called him an asshole. He told Gertrude what I said. She came after me with a broom. When I tried to block her from hitting me on my back, she hit my elbow instead. I screamed and my elbow started to bruise and swell up. I was in excruciating pain and could not move my arm. I just knew she broke it, and she thought so as well. She was scared and gave me a pack of ice to put on it. I felt I needed to go to the hospital then as well, but she refused to take me.

Every Thursday to get to choir rehearsal I caught the Greyhound bus across the street from my Erie Road home. I was too young to drive, so when I arrived at the Greyhound bus station Gertrude had a family friend pick me up from there and take me to my rehearsal. This friend really liked me, and Gertrude thought he was the perfect gentleman. I never liked him, and I made it known. He was extremely overweight and definitely not my type. But he knew the whereabouts of the girls' home that Gertrude sent Margaret to. So, I knew I had to be nice when I begged him to take me to see her. So, every Thursday I would visit her for about an hour before going to choir rehearsal. We promised each other we would never tell Gertrude our little secret.

Margaret moved back with us a few years later. We were both 18 and I had my driver's license. One day Lloyd and Gertrude allowed us to borrow the family van so we could visit Desiree in Buffalo. We were really going to visit her and our boyfriends whom we met together. Margaret and her friend separated from us. It was getting late, and I knew we had to be home by 11 p.m. I asked my friend if he knew where they may have gone to. I knew I could not leave without her, so I kept looking. She finally came back, but by the time we drove thirty miles to get home, the sun was rising. I said, "Please tell me that's the moon shining and not the sun coming up." The sun was shining when we pulled into the driveway. Lloyd and Gertrude were waiting up for us. They were angry when they said, "What do you think the neighbors are saying about you two?" "What kind of church girls stay out all night?" I said to myself, *we really don't have neighbors*. I had to give them my driver's license. I was sleepy but happy when Diane called and asked if I could come over and babysit.

Buffalo is known for its horrible snowstorms. One Saturday afternoon in December of 1978, Gertrude wanted us to drive to our church to drop off flowers that she had crocheted for the choir. She said they needed them that night. Margaret still did not have her license, so I had to drive. The roads were clear when we left the house. But, within fifteen minutes, the snow started blowing and causing whiteouts. I was driving about ten miles an hour when I hit a patch of black ice. I lost control of the van. We started sliding across the highway headed towards a ditch. I knew I had to steer the car in the direction of the slide to regain control. I managed to get the van in the right direction, but we were still sliding. I maneuvered the van towards an office building and parking lot, but it kept sliding.

I was terrified but knew I needed to be calm. Margaret, on the other hand, was screaming, grabbing my arm, and saying, "We're gonna crash! We're gonna die!" We slid into the parking lot and kept sliding toward the brick building. All I could think of was to call on Jesus. When I started praying, the van stopped within two inches of crashing into the building. Margaret was still crying, screaming, and holding my arm. I had to slap some sense into her and tell her to shut up. We never made it to the church. I drove back home and told Lloyd and Gertrude what happened. We were both visibly shaken up and scared. I really felt we were going to crash and die that day.

After several years, Lloyd and Gertrude finally lost their court battle for 363 Maiden Lane. It was sold for back taxes and 10880 became our permanent home. The only children around during that time were Alan, Corey, and me. Margaret was in and out. Gertrude decided to foster three more children. Two of the three were a brother and sister duo, 7-year-old Stacey, and her 5-year-old brother, Michael. The other was a ten-year-old chubby boy, named Bobby.

I was in my Junior year at S.U.N.Y. Oneonta in the Spring of 1982, when I received a phone call from Margaret telling me that our house had caught on fire. She said Gertrude had suffered smoke inhalation and was in the hospital. That following day, I took a Greyhound bus home, but she was out of the hospital when I arrived that evening. Loretta was stationed in California when her Commanding Officer informed her about the incident. She immediately took a flight to Buffalo and drove to Farnham, where they were staying in a hotel. She handed Gertrude $1000 in cash.

When I inquired about how the fire started, Gertrude said she was sewing and sent Stacey down to the basement to look for a pattern. While she was in the cluttered basement, she heard one of the kittens and wanted to find it. The light did not light up the entire basement, so she lit a piece of paper with matches that were found next to the furnace. The paper started burning, so she dropped it, ran back upstairs, and closed the door. She never said anything to anyone. The basement was on fire as the family went about their way. Gertrude started smelling the smoke and eventually saw it. She called 911 after everyone was safe and out of the house. She tried grabbing what she could, which caused her to suffer a little smoke inhalation. When the fire department arrived, they tried to help her, but Sheba, our German Shepard, would not allow the paramedics or firefighters near her.

The fire destroyed the home and all the belongings, except the family Bible, which I had bought for them a few years earlier. The large white Bible had a picture of who the publisher depicted as Jesus Christ. I dedicated the Bible, which they had sitting on one of their nightstands, to Gertrude and Lloyd. That same nightstand was completely burnt, but the Bible was only burnt around the edges, and it did not suffer water damage from them putting the fire out. Gertrude still has the Bible. She likes to tell everyone how the Bible was the only thing that was not destroyed by the fire and water.

The house and foundation were demolished and replaced with a two-bedroom mobile home donated by the Red Cross. Our church and community donated clothes, money, dishes, food, and many other needed items. Lloyd and Gertrude still had their motor home, which they slept in. Family Services had to remove the three younger foster children, but Margaret, Alan, and Corey were able to remain living there.

Lloyd suffered a heart attack that same year. It was a warm summer day when he woke up and told Gertrude he needed to go to the store. He was not feeling well and knew something was wrong. He did not want to alarm her, so he got in the van and drove himself to the hospital. He later told us that when he arrived at the hospital, he saw several nurses outside the door and drove as close to them as possible. They noticed him immediately and could see he was having a heart attack. Gertrude was sitting at the kitchen table, looking out the window, wondering where he was. She had no way of contacting him. She called his brother, Ben; but he had not heard from him either. Several hours later, our grandmother came over and Gertrude asked her if she knew where Lloyd was. Esther told her that Lloyd had the hospital staff call her. She knew he had suffered a heart attack, but said he was feeling a little chest congestion and wanted to go to the hospital. She said there was nothing to worry about and that the doctors would call her. Gertrude had recently undergone gallstone surgery and was unable to leave the house. Lloyd had to stay there for several weeks after having triple bypass surgery. He was unable to work for the City of Buffalo again.

They had a longtime friend, who we called Mr. Saul. While Lloyd was at work, he would come from Buffalo just about every morning with pastries to have coffee with Gertrude. He came over one day when I was there alone. He said he wanted to come in and wait for Gertrude. I told him I had no idea when she was coming back. While he was waiting, he started telling me how pretty I was, and he remembered when I was just a little girl. He then reached into his pocket, pulled out a $100 bill, and placed it on the table. He told me there was more to come, but I could not say anything to anybody, especially to Lloyd and Gertrude. I said okay and he left. Our parents never talked to any of us about these types of situations and what we needed to do when they occurred. I just knew he was wrong. When Gertrude came home, I explained what happened and gave her the money. I never saw him again.

It was April 1983 when I returned home from college. I was six months pregnant and dreaded every minute of having to go back to Lloyd and Gertrude's house. Margaret was there and pregnant as well. We both endured negative comments from them. She left and moved in with her child's father. After I had my baby, I decided I would join the Navy to be with my sister Loretta.

When I started the Navy enlistment process, the recruiter showed me a short film where recruits were forced into the deep end of a swimming pool. I could not swim and after a few near-drowning experiences, I knew that was not the right choice for me. I picked up my belongings and went next door to the Army recruiter.

When I left for the Army on January 19, 1983, I had no choice but to leave Jeffrey in Lloyd and Gertrude's custody. I returned five months later, after completing my basic training and advanced individual training (AIT). I was in disbelief when the Army would not allow Jeffrey to go to Germany with me. I was told single parents were not allowed to take their children overseas. Once again, Jeffrey needed to stay in Lloyd and Gertrude's custody.

When they renewed their vows for their 30th wedding anniversary, I was able to take leave and go to Buffalo for two weeks. I was happy to see some of my foster siblings. Then I returned to Germany, met my husband, got married, and gave birth to my second son. Several months later, I returned to the States and waited for my husband to join us.

Detroit Street

Lloyd and Gertrude had lost the 10880 property, as well. I could not understand how that happened after I took out a loan to help them rebuild the house. Someone they knew rented them a small apartment above a garage on Detroit Street in Farnham. Shortly thereafter, Lloyd and Gertrude relocated to Hampton, Virginia, leaving Alan behind. Corey was away at college. *Gertrude was motivated to move because she believed she had found her long-lost rich Uncle in Hampton.*

Lloyd passed away in March 2001. To date, as of 2024, Gertrude is still living in Hampton near Diane and her children. I decided to end all communication with them several years ago.

6

My Search Continues

Meeting my mother was bittersweet. I was happy to finally know who she was, but I still needed to complete my biological puzzle. I left for the Army, still not knowing too much about my birth father. No matter what I did or where I went, finding my father was always in the back of my mind. I wondered if I had any brothers, sisters, cousins, aunts, and uncles. *What about my grandparents? I needed to know where I belonged. Where did I come from? Was anyone looking for me, as well?* I had so many questions, with very few answers.

According to our conversation on the day we met, I felt my mother was out of the picture. I took the little information she shared with me and continued my search. I was now married with two sons, which made time for searching a little difficult. In 1987, I moved to Hampton, Virginia hoping my relationship with my foster parents would improve. I was also finishing my reserve duty obligation with the 88th Military Police Unit. I started searching once again, with the determination to never stop until I found the truth. Finding answers was extremely important to me and my family. It was difficult to answer health questions from our doctors. Whenever I was asked if certain diseases or health issues were common in my family history, I couldn't answer. I had no choice but to say, I grew up in foster care. It was hard and embarrassing to look at anyone and say I don't know. I also wondered if any health issues ran anywhere in my family that could possibly affect me and my children.

All I knew was that I was looking for someone named Billy, who played drums for Grover Washington, Jr. in 1960. He was eighteen years old and lived with his aunt. That was all the information I had to go on. I started my research with Grover and found that he was a jazz musician who was born and raised in Buffalo. I heard about him through Gertrude. I was excited when my internet research found a drummer named Billy who played for Grover. I continued researching him. I knew Hampton University had a jazz radio station, so I called to ask if they had any albums by this now-famous jazz drummer. They did and I went to see what information I could get off the album. It had a picture of two girls that I thought looked like me. I was able to borrow it for a few days.

Excitement, filled with determination, took over. I was working for the Central Accounting Office at Fort Monroe, Virginia. I took the album with me to show my good friend and co-worker, Donna Kelly. I needed her to help me find his contact information and there was nothing on the album. The record label information was printed on the back with their address and phone number, which was in New York. I did not have a long-distance phone service at home, so I made all my calls from work. *I figured they would never know.* I called and spoke to a male representative. When I explained that I was a family member, and it was imperative that I speak with this Billy person, he did not hesitate to give me his phone number. The number he gave me was for Italy. I knew I could get fired if I called from work. I was able to use my neighbor's long-distance phone service who kept in touch with her family living in Japan.

When I called the number, I listened to a recording of a man's voice saying he was not at home and gave me another number to contact him. I asked the operator which country I was calling this time. She said Switzerland.

The phone rang twice before he answered it with a deep hello. I knew I had to keep calm. I said hello in my cheery voice, "My name is Judy Welch and I live in Hampton, Virginia, but I was born and raised in Buffalo, New York." I told him my story and what my mother had said to me about my biological father. Then, I asked him if he knew my mother, Judith Levisy, and he said not that he remembered. I started asking him questions about the album I was holding in my hand. I felt it was strange that he was unable to answer any of my questions. When I finished talking, he started laughing at me. I could not believe he felt this matter was a joke. I said, "There is nothing funny about this at all. If you are my father, I don't want anything from you. I am a married woman with children of my own and I just want the satisfaction of knowing where I came from." He said, "I don't think I am the person you are looking for but give me your name and number and I will see if I can help." So, I did as he asked. We never spoke again, in person, that is.

I believed that Billy was indeed my father. He played drums for Grover, just like my mom said. He wasn't honest with me when I questioned him about the album, which led me to believe he was, but did not want to admit it. I left comments on his MySpace page, hoping he would respond; instead, I was blocked. I had to find another way. Even though my mom and I were not communicating, I decided to call her. To my surprise, she answered. I told her I was still looking for my dad and had found a drummer named Billy. I asked her, "Please go to Record Theater there in Buffalo, look at the album, and let me know if it was him." She said, "Yes," and told me she would call me back the following Tuesday. Well, I waited. She did call back on Tuesday, but it was three months later. She told me, "No, that was not him." I asked her again if there was anything else she could remember. It was always the same. His name was Billy and he played drums. This time, she said, "If you really want to know who your father is, you need to contact Grover Washington, Jr." Several years passed before we spoke again.

My family and I moved to Chicago in the summer of 1992. The Oprah Winfrey Show was airing, and I knew she could help me find the answers if I could just speak with her or a producer. But my calls and letters went unanswered.

Several more years passed by, but I refused to give up. I had the right to know. I called my mother again and to my surprise, my sister, Julie, answered the phone. I told her who I was. She said her mother was not home, so we talked for a while. I told her my story, because I wanted her to know about me and that I was not trying to cause any trouble. I was just looking for my dad and I needed Judy to give me more information. She did say her mom had told her about me. We spoke several more times after that. I was also able to have several conversations with Judy's now ex-husband, Ziggy, from Dunkirk. He reassured me that he was not racist.

Julie and her father were instrumental in starting the conversations between Judy and me. We started talking again, which gave room for the two of us to finally start building a lasting relationship. I wanted her to know that I harbored no hard feelings towards her.

In 2001, I was working as a legal secretary for a law firm in Chicago. I expressed to my boss that I wanted to take my sons on a vacation to Buffalo, Niagara Falls, and Canada to show them where I grew up. He surprised me with an extra vacation bonus and said, "Have fun!" I was excited when I told Julie, Ziggy, and Judy that we were going to be in Buffalo for a week and would love to see them. But there was one other person I had not spoken to yet… my brother Joey. We were finally able to talk over the phone a week before my trip. He said that Judy told him about me two days prior. They had a conversation, where she told him he had another sister. He was excited to know that but wondered why she never told him and Julie before then. She said, "There's one other thing. She's Black." He said he did not care about my race and wanted to know more about me. She told him I was coming to Buffalo, and he would be able to meet me in a week. I was a little surprised to hear she waited so long to tell them about me when I knew about them in 1985.

I had not seen Judy in over 16 years. Plus, I was meeting my brother, sister, and their dad for the first time. I was nervous and wondered how everyone was going to react. My sons knew they had a Caucasian grandmother, but I was still concerned about their reactions. But only Judy, Joey, and Ziggy met us at the hotel. I was disappointed when I did not see Julie. Joey said she was too nervous to go with them. I could not understand why, when she was the main person, I had talked to. I thought maybe I was too direct, and it scared her. I did not want her or anyone in that family to fear anyone in mine. That was not my intention. Mom later said Julie was unable to get off work.

I introduced my sons, and everyone greeted each other with smiles and hugs. My nervousness subsided when I realized we were going to be okay. I must say, we had an awesome time together. Judy brought a box full of old family photos. She gave me a few of her mother, her and Ziggy's wedding, as well as pictures of Julie and Joey when they were much younger. She asked the boys about school and their grades. Joey, Ziggy, and I had great conversations with each other. We took plenty of pictures, as we enjoyed each other's company.

We all had other plans for the day and had to say goodbye, a few hours later. The hours we spent together were meaningful, heartfelt, and precious to me. To my surprise, neither one of us mentioned anything regarding my father.

Judy and I stayed in touch and communicated as much as we could. It was difficult to call her "Mom," especially since I was still talking and visiting Lloyd and Gertrude in Virginia. At that time, I felt Gertrude would feel betrayed. So, I only called Judy, Mom, when no one else was listening.

Another fifteen years passed before we would see each other again in July 2016. My foster sister, Diane, had a party in Buffalo to celebrate her 60th birthday. I called Judy to give her the dates I was going to be there. I could hear the excitement in her voice. She planned a dinner with family members that I still needed to meet. Over twenty relatives were waiting for me at the restaurant. Unfortunately, I was not able to go. My plane arrived an hour late. Diane, Gertrude, and their friends picked me up from the airport. I explained to them that Judy and some of my family members were waiting for me at the restaurant and I needed to be there. Diane was driving and said we didn't have time because we needed to be at Corey's house. I was extremely upset because I had told them my plans a few weeks before the trip. They purposely arranged their schedule, to avoid me seeing my real family. I had no choice but to call Judy to explain why I was unable to attend, and I could hear the disappointment in her voice. I wanted to leave Diane and rent my own car.

I felt bad and needed to find a way to make it up to my family. Judy and I made plans to meet for breakfast the following day. She was able to re-gather as many family members as she could, but a few were unable to attend. I was finally able to meet my beautiful sister Julie and her boyfriend (now husband) Steven. The first thing she said to him was, "She looks like Mom." We held hands as we stared at each other for a few seconds, trying not to cry. Then my Aunt Andrea gave me the biggest hug and said, "I thought I would never see this day."

There were cousins, husbands, girlfriends, and boyfriends coming to meet me. I cried and hugged every one of them before we sat down to eat. I could not believe that I was sitting around a long table, eating breakfast with my biological family. We exchanged social media information and phone numbers and vowed to stay in touch. I will never forget that amazing day!

7

It's Over!

Everything was going well with Mom and my Buffalo family. But I still felt something was missing. I could not stop thinking about the other half of my DNA. I heard about two DNA websites but found them to be a bit costly. One evening, I saw an Ancestry commercial. They were offering a Mother's Day special for only $59. I wanted to make sure they were legit, and I figured if they were advertising on television, they had to be trustworthy. I went to their website and placed an order; not just for me, but also for my sister Loretta. It was my Mother's Day gift to her and myself!

I received my kit two weeks later and mailed it back the following day. I followed their instructions by filling out my profile on their website; so, when the results came in, I would receive an email. It took five weeks before I received any notification.

Finally on July 14, 2020, at 8:21 a.m., I received an email with the subject Your AncestryDNA results are in! I was nervous and excited at the same time. As I started navigating through it, I was really surprised to see my results. I come from twelve world regions. I can finally put aside my belief in the person who I thought was my dad. His region was not listed. There were so many faces and names that matched from both sides. I knew the white relatives were on my mom's side. There was a lot of history for me to explore, and that's what I did. I found it all to be intriguing.

I received my first message that same day from Aaron Whitaker! It showed our DNA proved we were third cousins. I responded with my number, and we spoke for hours trying to see if we had other common relatives. His great-grandfather was Herbert Smith. Herbert's oldest daughter Lilybell married Haywood Wilkins. They had a daughter named Judy, who is Aaron's mom. We called each other every day for several months to say hello. Aaron lives with his beautiful wife, Phalencia, in North Carolina. We still communicate when time permits.

I immediately started sending messages that same day, hoping other people would respond. My main focus was on relatives with the closest DNA match. Pamela Marie Smith, a second cousin, replied five days later. We talked just about every day for hours. I told her my story; she began researching and calling other relatives. When she realized that I was indeed an unknown family member, she welcomed me and said that I am part of a large, loving, and God-fearing family whose last name is Smith. The Smiths are originally from the Tarbert Plantation in Wilkinson County, Mississippi. My Great Grandparents were Gus and Rose (Anderson) Smith. They had twelve children - six boys and six girls. The family remained living and working on the plantation when slavery was abolished. In July 1878, when the worst epidemic of yellow fever became widespread, the family moved to New Orleans. When Hurricane Katrina devastated that area, many of the families relocated to Texas and a few other states, as well. Cousin Pamela saw the picture I put on Ancestry and said I look like her Aunt Renetta, who was her father's youngest sister.

Tarbert Plantation was located in Wilkinson County, Mississippi. It's interesting to note that this plantation experienced a cholera outbreak in 1849, during which 30 slaves tragically lost their lives to the disease. Unfortunately, specific details about its exact location are not entirely clear, but it was situated somewhere in Wilkinson County. The historical context of plantations like Tarbert sheds light on the complex and often tragic history of the American South.

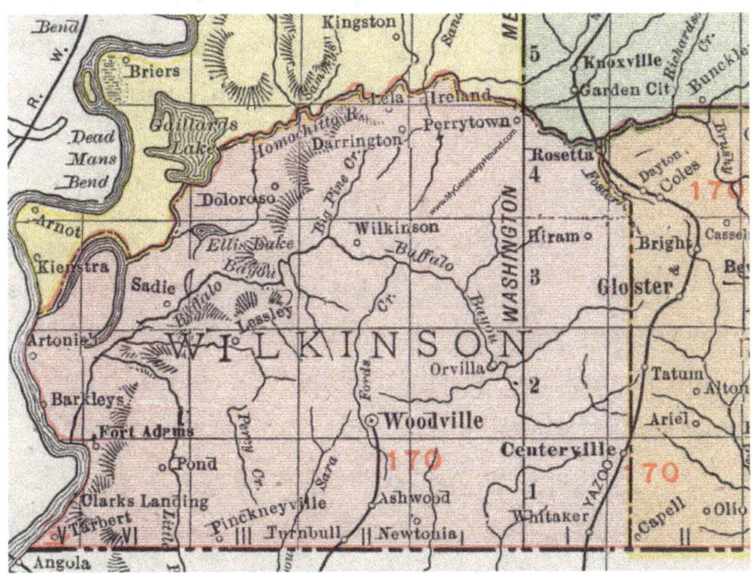

Tarbert Plantation, Wilkinson County MS

I received another message the same day from Jacquelyn Smith Bearden, first cousin, one time removed. When I told her my story, she told me the same thing that Pam said about the family. They both welcomed me and expressed how excited they were to have my family be a part of theirs. All I could do was cry when I felt the sincerity in their voices. I knew they meant what they said. As they spread the word about me to their families, we worked together to find more answers to questions I had been searching for, year after year. I felt in my heart I was getting closer to knowing who my dad was. Everything was pointing back to their Aunt Renetta. Pamela and Jacquelyn called other family members to see if any of the original twelve had a son named Billy. It was not hard to do because only five of the twelve had children. They were told Aunt Renetta had three sons - Bertron, Jozell, and Adrian. I was asking myself, *can one of them be my father?* When they asked their older relatives about her sons, they were told she had sent Bertron and Jozell to live with two of her sisters in Buffalo at an early age.

At this point, it was confirmed that I am a Smith family member and I do look like Aunt Renetta when she was younger. *But who and where is this Billy person that my mom told me about?* I knew my mother's birthday, and that Billy was a year older. I did more research on Ancestry to pinpoint the birthdays of Aunt Renetta's sons while Pamela and Jacquelyn continued their search, as well. I found a wealth of information.

Our research revealed Aunt Renetta's middle son, Jozell, matched the age bracket with her. I asked my mom, "If I send you a picture, will you be able to identify him?" She said yes. I could tell from her voice that she was a little nervous. I texted her a picture that Cousin Jacquelyn sent me of my potential father, she texted back with, *yes, that was him.*

On July 23, 2020, at 9:15 a.m. the search for my biological father ended. There I was, texting my mother while looking at a picture of my father. I started rejoicing and thanking GOD. My 42-year search was finally over. I told my mom that his real name was not Billy. She asked, "Where is he now?" I had to tell her the truth. Her words to me were, "Well, you have come a long way. Glad you finally got closure." I knew she was happy for me. But I will never get closure with my dad because I never met him.

My father's name was Jozell Saintamaer Blake, born September 19, 1942, in Buffalo. In January 1962, he changed his name to Jozell S. Carter. He lived with his aunt and played drums for Grover. He was seventeen when he met my mom at one of his performances. Billy was his stage name. Now the pieces of the puzzle fit together. Pamela and Jacquelyn's Aunt Renetta was my paternal grandmother. She passed away on August 10, 2005, in Huntsville, Alabama.

I have no choice but to take the bitter with the sweet, once again. Unfortunately for me, I will never have an opportunity to meet him or build a father-daughter relationship. My research revealed that the father I had been searching for all those years passed away on Father's Day June 20, 2004, in Indianapolis, Indiana. He was only 61 years old. I started to wonder about many things. I felt I missed out on knowing what kind of person he was, and wished I could have found him sooner.

While Pamela and Jacquelyn continued gathering information, I continued with my research. I found his death certificate which listed his daughter Giselle as next of kin. I was excited to know I had a younger sister. My cousins shared his obituary, which revealed he had two daughters instead of one, Giselle Carter Williams and Pamela Carter Roach, as well as a son, Kevin Price. I was excited to hear about them, but those three siblings had no idea I existed. I really wanted to get to know them but was not sure how they would react. I started to wonder if they would even want to get to know me and my family. Pamela and Jacquelyn shared more information about my new family. They helped me to understand the family tree by sending pictures and naming family members, young and old alike.

I had two uncles. My oldest uncle was living in Buffalo when he passed away. He and my aunt had three children. My youngest uncle, Adrian Watkins, had three children, as well. I was told he lived in California. His son was on Ancestry, and it showed we were first cousins. I messaged him and waited for his reply. We lived only twenty-four miles apart.

My new Cousin Pamela called me on July 24th and said, "I think I know who your sisters are!" She sent me a picture of them, taken at the family reunion, standing with our Uncle Adrian. I stared at that picture and cried. The joy I was feeling at that moment was overwhelming in a good way. In just a matter of days, my background came together. I was looking at two beautiful ladies that looked like me. I knew I had to meet them and was hoping they felt the same way. Cousin Pamela contacted my sister, Pamela, and told her about me. Sister Pamela called Giselle and told her the news. On July 26, 2020, my sisters and I talked for six straight hours. There were so many questions, as expected.

One of the first things they said was, "There is no inheritance." I knew they thought I was looking for something from them, which was not the case. I started the conversation by reassuring them that I was not looking for anything but the satisfaction of knowing where I came from. I told them about me and what my mom shared about my father, including the part where he got another girl pregnant at the same time. I bought the Ancestry kit, hoping I could find some answers. They wanted to know more about Ancestry and how it worked. I shared my DNA results and how they matched me with other family members who were registered with Ancestry. We all know DNA does not lie. I explained how Pamela and Jacqueline connected with me.

Pamela said she saw me on one of my social media pages, looked at my sons, and knew it was true. Giselle on the other hand was very skeptical and wanted more proof. I told them both that I would be willing to pay for their kits. Giselle received her results first and was excited to know the truth.

My sisters shared that our dad's number one priority was his music. That was at the sacrifice of his family because his music came first. There were a lot of broken promises he often made to his daughters. He promised to visit them in Buffalo, but never did. The joyful times they remember were visits to the zoo and with their Aunt Lula and Aunt Carrie. They were excited to attend his recordings and would invite their friends to join them. They were proud of him and his musical accomplishments. He loved dogs and often picked up strays, bought them food, or took them home. He had a love for all types of food and was not afraid to try anything. He was a serious foodie, and the hotter, the better it was for him. He also loved to go fishing.

They said that even though he was not in their lives, they had a desire to have him walk them down the aisle on the most important day of their young lives. It was not easy for them to get to that point, due to his too many broken promises. He became a doting dad and grandfather. He planned to spend time with his grandchildren. It was like he wanted to make up for the times he missed with his daughters. He believed in the value of relationships, with anyone and everyone. He knew people by name and people knew him everywhere he traveled.

8

All Together Now!

The emptiness and void of not knowing where I belong is now filled with love that barely existed. Through the years, I met several of my maternal relatives. It was now time for my paternal side. I was ready to meet and greet as many relatives as I could. But we were at the beginning of a horrific pandemic that hindered any of us from coming together. Public transportation came to a standstill, and everyone was in quarantine. The hope of visiting my family became impossible. Here I am, knowing the truth, but unable to physically embrace it!

We did what we could to stay connected. My siblings and I periodically called each other and sent text messages. We were hoping to come together for our first holiday dinner. But COVID made it impossible, so my sisters and I decided to prepare our Thanksgiving dinner via video. We were on the call for several hours, talking, laughing, and cooking while giving each other tips. It was amazing.

Later that night I met my first Cousin, Dawn (Sherry), on a Zoom call. Even though Giselle told her my story, she still had some doubts and a lot of questions to ask. I reassured her that I was not looking for any inheritance of any kind. I had already found what I was looking for.

Every time I met someone new, they wanted to hear my story. So many cousins were excited to meet me and my family. Giselle, with the help of Pamela and Jacquelyn, contacted all the family members they could and arranged a video conference call for November 27, 2020. Everybody was smiling and excited to meet me and my family. They introduced themselves and said who they were the descendants of. I was able to look at their family tree beforehand which gave me a better understanding, as well. Afterward, we had several more video calls. I started receiving emails with pictures and calls from new cousins. They were sharing their stories and wanted to know more about mine. I should have recorded it and played it back every time someone new called.

Some people started traveling again in 2021. I just happened to be visiting my sister, Loretta in Las Vegas at the same time my cousin, Crystal, and her husband, Thaddeus, were visiting from Chicago. We met on February 22nd. We had lunch and then went shoe shopping. They were the first family members I met in person.

2022 was an even better year. I was so excited to finally meet my Uncle Adrian and his family. He invited us to a luncheon in Long Beach to help celebrate family members with January birthdays. We came together on January 30, 2022. I was excited and nervous as my sons and I, their significant others, and my grandchildren walked towards the clubhouse. It was a special moment and I wanted others to share it with me, so I went live on social media. My family started filming again when my uncle greeted us at the bottom of the stairs. I started crying as we stood there embracing each other. My dad was not alive, but I felt he was hugging me through his brother. It was a spiritual moment. Something I thought I would never experience. I met the rest of my cousins and their children. My uncle had a few of his closest friends joining in on the celebration. Dawn (Sherry) came from Las Vegas with her brother from Orange County. My uncle gave everyone birthday gifts, including three of my family members. We all ate, took pictures, and talked for several hours, just getting to know one another.

My beautiful sister, Julie, had planned her wedding, but due to the pandemic, she was forced to postpone it for a year. I was so excited to finally be able to go back to Buffalo in June for her Princess wedding. I had not seen my mom, Julie, and Joey since 2016. My cousins and aunt whom I met then were excited to see me. I was happy to meet my brother-in-law Steven's family as well. I must say, some people were a little shocked when I introduced myself as Julie's sister. The look on their faces made me laugh to myself because I knew they had no idea she had a Black sister. On the day of her wedding, I was escorted down the aisle to sit in the front row behind the bridesmaids. As I was sitting down, the photographer approached me and said in an unpleasant tone, "I see you are wearing a flower. Who are you?" I could see other guests staring and waiting for my response. I politely said with a smile, "I'm Judy, Julie's sister." She said, "Oh," and walked away. Her body language showed how shocked she was at my answer. I looked around and smiled, as I sat in my designated seat. I never felt uncomfortable because I knew I belonged there.

On the morning that I arrived, Mom met me at my hotel and took me to one of her favorite restaurants for breakfast. She introduced me as her daughter from Los Angeles. On my last day in Buffalo, both of us went shopping together for the very first time. We went back to her apartment for a few hours and sang along with oldies but goodies music. It was a wonderful mother/daughter memorable moment. I cried that night as I left for the airport, thinking about her and how much I admired her for loving me. My tears were joyful ones because I knew she was not ashamed of giving me life. I wanted her to be proud of me, as I was of her, and always will be.

I had other reasons for going to Buffalo, as well. I was there to finally meet my brother, Kevin Price. We were born the same year and are only six months apart. We had spoken several times since our sister Giselle told him about me in 2020. I was craving Buffalo wings, so we met at the Anchor Bar, home of the famous wings. Kevin and I spent several hours together as we shared our life stories. He felt he had a good relationship with Dad. Though he wasn't in his life growing up, Kevin could still see some of himself in our father. He told me about Dad's days when he played drums for a group called "Speak Easy," which often appeared at "The Pine Grill" in Buffalo. In 2003, they had a chance to bridge the gaps in their relationship.

We took pictures as we walked along the waterfront. I followed him to the Tops supermarket where ten people had recently lost their lives. It was a solemn moment as I stood there looking at hundreds of flowers, stuffed animals, candles, and pictures. We later went to our aunt's home, where I was able to see some pictures of our father and other family members taken throughout the years.

I was not going to leave Buffalo without finding my sister, Margaret. I had spoken to Walt and my nieces before I left Los Angeles, to inform them I was coming and wanted to take them out to eat. Walt agreed to help me find Margaret and had a general idea of her whereabouts. I drove out to Dunkirk. Unfortunately, he was unable to get my nieces and their families together all at once. When I arrived at Walt's home, I saw Shaniece and her lovely daughters first. My nieces were teenagers when I last saw them. We were excited to finally see each other again. Shay, as we call her, is a nurse. We left Walt's house to look for Margaret. I was hoping we would find her, so she could eat with us. We drove around to various locations where he had spotted her several times before, but we were not able to find her. We then drove to the house where he would oftentimes see her sitting on the porch. We saw a guy sitting there instead. Walt and

I approached him and introduced ourselves. I told him I was looking for my sister, Margaret, and asked if he knew her. He said yes that she lived there but had just left walking down the street, and he had no idea when she was coming back. We exchanged numbers and he promised he would call or text me when she returned. He also said he would not tell her I came by, so it would be a surprise. I told him thank you and left. Walt, the girls, and I went to a nearby pizza restaurant on the waterfront. We took pictures by the water and went shopping for toys. Shaniece and her daughters left afterwards.

A few minutes later, the guy sent a text saying Margaret was back and we should come now. We parked in the lot next door. I asked Walt to walk ahead of me because I was so nervous and did not know what to expect. It had been over 20 years since the last time I saw my sister. She recognized him and they started talking. The guy said, "Come on, don't be scared." I walked closer and froze in place, as I kept looking at her. I could tell she had no idea who I was when she saw me. She said, "Who are you?" I said, "It's me, Judy, your sister." I had to repeat myself several times. She said, "No, it's not you." I shook my head, yes, and we both started crying. We hugged and did not want to let each other go. I told her that I came looking for her and was not leaving Buffalo until I found her. She asked how I knew where to find her. Walt told Margaret that he remembered seeing her several times, sitting on the porch. I was able to finally see my sister and let her know I never gave up looking for her. I told her how much I still loved her and would always be there. We took pictures and promised to keep in touch. We hugged again as tightly as we could and cried. I left there, wishing I could have brought her back with me.

I picked up Walt the following day so we could spend time with my other niece, Natisha, and her family. As we were driving through Angola, I told him that I wanted to stop by my high school to take a few pictures. As I stood in the parking lot, I thought about the racist students and teachers who tried to make our lives difficult. I said to myself *if only they could see me now.* We met Tisha at the same restaurant my mom took me to. We were so happy to see each other for the first time in twenty-two years. She introduced me to her husband and son, Jackson. We talked about our families and what they were all doing. Tisha, as we call her, is an entrepreneur. She makes beautiful porcelain jewelry and trinkets. We took lots of pictures before heading to the store to buy Jackson a toy. We said our goodbyes, promising to stay in touch.

I am very proud of my nieces and their accomplishments. They both have beautiful families, excellent careers, and positive attitudes. Margaret and I talk several times a week. She knows I will always be there for her. I can finally say we have that sister bond that was lost for years. I am looking forward to her coming to Los Angeles.

As we drove towards Walt's home, we stopped at what used to be 10880 Erie Road. There were so many tall trees and overgrown bushes. I knew where the house once stood, but I could not see anything. Even the driveway was covered. I stood there for a few minutes, took a couple of pictures, and drove away.

10880 Erie Road

We left there and drove a few yards towards Maiden Lane. So many thoughts and memories were coming to mind as we slowly drove down the dead-end road. The cows and fence that were usually on the right were long gone. As I looked to the left there was a small sign that read 345. I told Walt that was where my grandmother had lived. Her house was still standing as well as the little brick house. But tall grass and bushes blocked our view from seeing the pond and stream as we drove across the little bridge. The two-story house that once stood on 363 had fallen.

363 Maiden Lane (2024)

I could still see the frame of what used to be a house. The grass had grown over what was once the U-shaped driveway. The big cherry tree that stood in the middle, which Gertrude had used for switches, was cut down. The old rusty well, where we once pumped our water, had been removed. The barn that housed our horse and dogs was nowhere to be found. It looked empty, but the memories were full.

We noticed someone was watching us from a vehicle near the driveway at 345. The car drove towards us, and the female driver asked if she could help us. I told her my name and that my family used to live there in the 60s and 70s. I said my grandmother once lived in the house on 345. She then introduced herself as the owner of both properties. She wanted to show me the changes her husband made to the house they were living in. I followed her to 345 and immediately noticed a big Rottweiler on a chain. She said it was okay to get out of the car, he wouldn't bite. Walt and I looked at each other and said, "It's okay, we can see from here." When I said that I did not feel comfortable around her big dog, she had her son take it into the house and put him in his cage. She showed me the side of the house where they had replaced all the apple trees with an above-ground pool. The smaller sheds where the chickens once stayed were covered with bushes, trees, and tall grass. The tall pine tree that was in the center of the front yard had been replaced with a huge flower bush.

She wanted me to go in the house with her to see how her husband remodeled the kitchen several years ago, but I was too nervous because I knew her big dog was in there. Walt was just as scared as I was and stayed outside. I told him if I was not out in a few minutes or if he heard me scream, call 911. There was a lot of stuff on the floors, chairs, and cabinets, which made it difficult to see anything. I told her it looked great and headed back to the front door. I stopped at the living room doorway and to my surprise, the same wallpaper was still on the walls after all these years. However, I noticed where it started to peel in the upper corners. I told her that was the same wallpaper my grandmother had.

As we walked outside, I told her that, at one point I had considered buying back the property. She had planned to leave it to her sons, but they told her they wanted nothing to do with it. She said I would be the first person she would consider when the time comes. We exchanged numbers and I thanked her for her time. I must be honest with myself, regarding that property. I felt a little eerie standing on those grounds. The harsh memories overshadowed the beauty of the land. *I wondered if that's how former slaves felt when they returned to a plantation.*

I drove Walt home and thanked him for everything he did to help me find Margaret. I told him how proud I was of the wonderful job he did raising their daughters. He thanked me for coming and spending time with all of them.

As I headed back towards Buffalo, I needed to make one last stop that held a few more memories. I drove two miles down a long narrow road with freshly cut grass all around. I stopped in the big parking lot of Evangola State Park. The sun was starting to set, so I hurried down to the beach to get a few pictures of the Lake Erie sunset. As I looked around, I thought about the two summers I worked as a camp counselor. I thought about the time I almost drowned when the waves carried me out too far and I was unable to touch the bottom. I could still hear my brother Melvin telling me to walk backwards. As I watched the sunset for a few minutes, I was able to see Canada from a distance. I took a few more pictures and then drove back to my hotel.

Texas was my next trip!! After attending my first Mary Kay convention in August, I stayed in Dallas to finally meet my sisters, their families, and a few of my cousins living in the surrounding area. I took an Uber to their mother's home about an hour away.

I was nervous and excited to finally meet everyone in person. Momma Martha was waiting at her front door and greeted me with a big friendly smile and a hug. Once inside, she showed me family pictures of my sisters taken throughout the years. Giselle arrived shortly afterward. I stood there looking at her while saying to myself, *this is real. I am not dreaming.* When we arrived at her beautiful home, my brother-in-law, niece, and nephew were as excited to finally see me in person, as I was to see them. We had previously met during one of our Zoom calls. I stayed with Giselle for five days and had one of the best times getting to know more about her and the Smith family tree. The hot weather did not stop us from exploring Fort Worth and its surrounding areas. There was a lot of taxidermy in just about every place we entered. We watched herders walk the longhorn cattle through the stockyards. I thought it was exciting because I had never seen anything like that before. We later stopped at a BBQ restaurant to buy dinner. That was my first time eating Texas BBQ.

Giselle and Pam have some of Dad's items they hold dear to their hearts. Giselle showed me a few inside his trunk that came from the home he grew up in. The room where I slept was filled with his memories. There was a photo of him and décor from his last apartment in Indianapolis. She has his special set of orange drums that are extremely sentimental. I felt his presence as I looked at and held items he once had.

On August 4th, a few of my cousins wanted to have a little reunion with us. They suggested that everyone wear their orange T-shirt from the 2018 family reunion. We went to a nearby store to buy me one. Dinner was ready when our cousins Glenn Smith, Illona Smith, and Jacquelyn Smith Bearden arrived. I could not stop crying, with tears of gratitude and excitement, to see more of my father's family. My cousins presented me with an "official" family reunion T-shirt that I put on over the one I was wearing. I felt that family reunion T-shirt, as simple as it may seem, solidified me as an official Smith family member. We sat around the dining room table eating, laughing, and talking.

We later went outside and sat around the pool with our feet in the water. We did a little karaoke as we listened to music. My niece and nephew joined us for a few minutes, as well. We ate a little more, as we played "Heads Up." That was such a fun game to play. We sang and played, and played and sang. The time I spent with my sisters, their families, and our cousins meant so much to me. We shared quality time, getting to know each other. I left Texas the following day, feeling loved and appreciated by people like me. I thought about my father and wondered what my life would have been like if he had accepted me.

Yes, I know I missed out on making memories with both sides of my family; but I feel it's never too late to create new ones. 2022 was the year that GOD helped me to do just that, for the first time. I refused to give up searching for the truth. I knew it was out there somewhere, and it took me forty-two years to find it. I owe it all to HIM!!!

Epilogue
Celebrating Jeffrey

The death of my oldest son, Jeffrey Levisy, was extremely hard on all of us as a family. He died from a heart attack caused by an enlarged heart at the early age of twenty-two.

I don't say I lost my son because I know where he is. "He just beat me to heaven." We come together every year on March 18th, which is the day he passed; and on his birthday July 20th to celebrate his memory. We cherish a few of his personal belongings.

Conclusion

My life has not always been easy. I had many challenges that tried to block my blessings, but I knew I could not give up. I was given seven days to live, when I became sick with meningitis in 1997, and I survived ovarian cancer in 2004. I never forget who GOD is and what HE has done for me, so I could not give up. There is no failure in HIM.

The many situations and circumstances I faced throughout my life have prepared me to be the person I am today. I survived domestic violence when I divorced my children's father. I did not want my sons to grow up, believing that's how they should treat a female.

My sons, Andre, Tim, and Chris are living successfully in the Southern California area, near me. I am extremely proud of their accomplishments and the goals they set out to achieve. We have a close bond that some people do not understand why and how. I thank GOD for allowing me to be their mother, for they have been the wind beneath my wings.

*She was 8 months old when she arrived at
17 Viola Park, dressed in a pink bunny snowsuit.
This is ...*

JUDITH LEVISY'S

PHOTO JOURNEY

I'LL ALWAYS CHERISH MY FOSTER SISTERS

Me and My Sisters - Margaret and Loretta.
"Grandma" Esther would buy all of us new clothes every Easter.

Family Trip to Buffalo (2001)

Me and My Sister Loretta

Loretta & Her Late Husband Mitch

Me and Margaret (2001)and (2022)

Me, Walt, my neice Tisha, and her son (Buffalo, June 2022)

Walt, my niece Shay, and daughters (June 2022)

Evangola State Park Sunset (June 2022)

One of my original oil paintings

High School (1979)

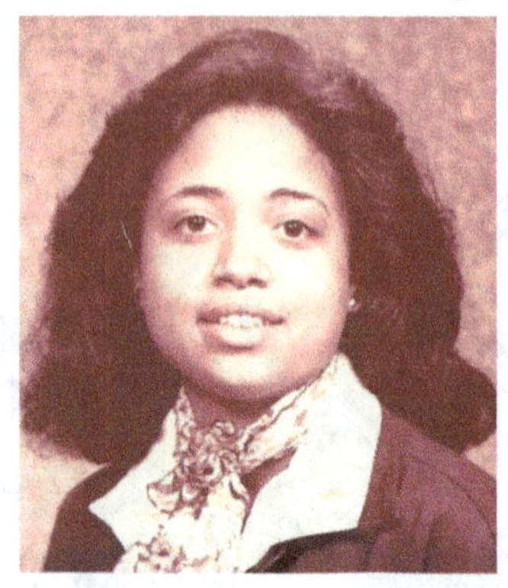

Oneonta Fashion Show and Play

Me, Donna Kelly and Fort Monroe Accounting

Basic Training and AIT Graduation

Basic Training Graduation - March 23, 1984

AIT Graduation – May 16, 1984

My Graduation (May 2019)

Veterans Empowerment Theater

Tim's Graduation (June 2021)

My Sister Loretta and Daughter-In-Law Felicia at my 60th Birthday Party

My Daughters In-Law, Felicia and Jennifer at my 60th Birthday Party

*My 60th Birthday with my sons, Andre and Tim in Long Beach
(May 2021)*

FINALLY.....FAMILY TIES
Maternal Family

Me, my brother Joey, and Mom (June 2022)   *Me and Mom (June 2022)*

My Grandparents, Harry and Marie Levisy

Lunch with my Levisy Family (July 2016)

A few cousins I met at Julie's Wedding (June 2022)

My sister Julie's Wedding (June 2022)

FINALLY.....FAMILY TIES
Paternal Family

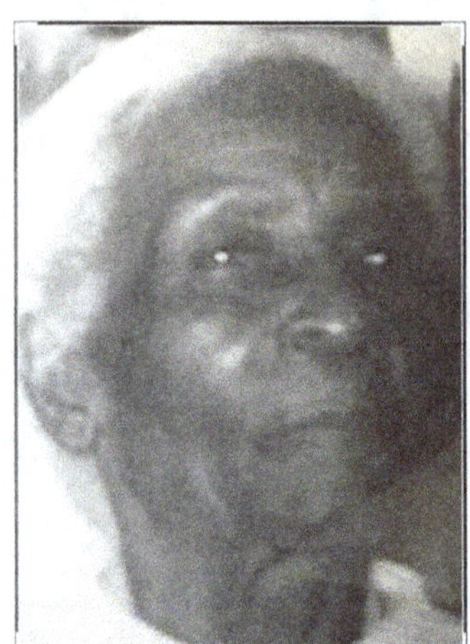

Great Grandfather, Gus Smith Sr.   Great Grandmother, Rose Smith

Grandma Renetta and her sons - Uncle Adrian, Dad, and Uncle Bert

Aunt Carrie, Grandma Renetta & Aunt Luticia

My Grandfather, John Carter

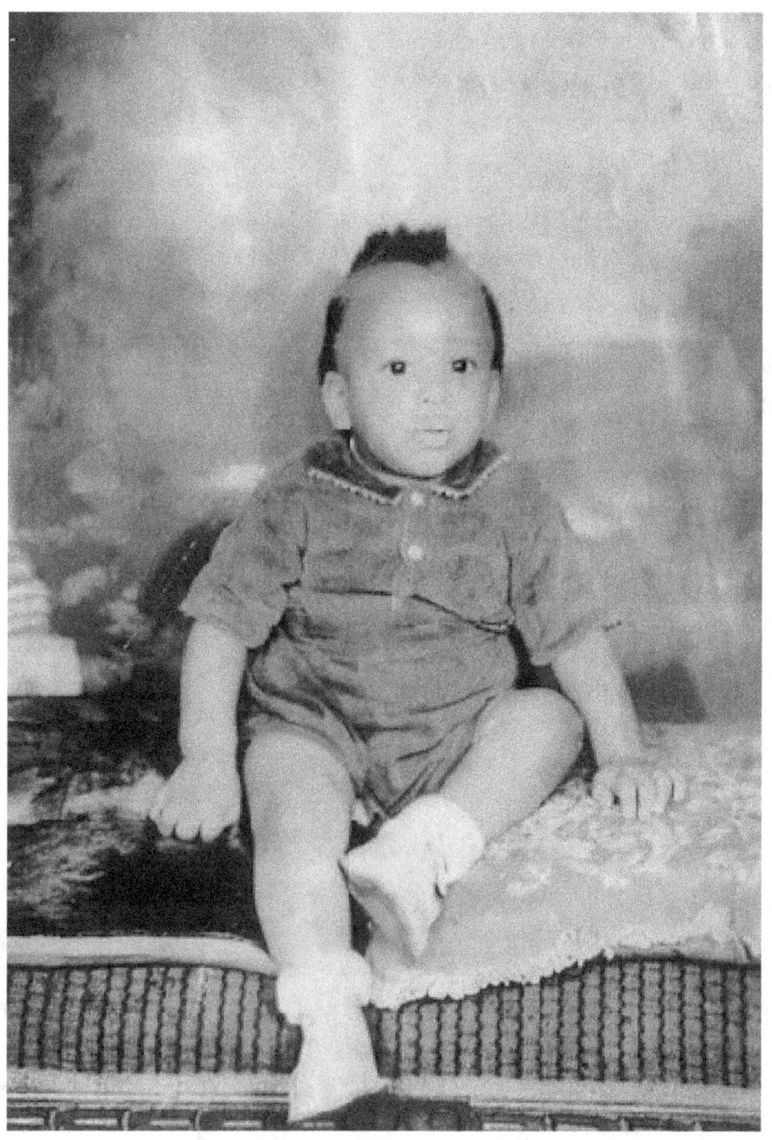

Baby Jozelle Carter (My Dad)

Grandma Renetta

Great-grandmother Rose and Her 6 Daughters and Grandson

Back Row - Grandma Renetta and her sisters: Great Aunts Carrie, Rose, Luticia, Ida, and Mary
Front Row - Uncle Bert and Great-Grandmother Rose

Great Grandparents with Their 6 Sons

Top, left to right - Great Uncles: Paul Sr, Estevan Sr, Pastor James, Freddie Sr, Nathan Gus Jr
Botton, left to right – Oliver (Son of Paul Sr) My Uncle Bert, Great Grandmother Rose Anderson Smith, Great Grandfather Gus Smith, and Ernest (son of Paul Sr)

DISCOVERING THE DAD I NEVER KNEW...

R.I.P

Jozelle Saintamaer Blake was born on September 19, 1942, in Buffalo. In January 1962, he changed his name to Jozelle S. Carter. Regrettably, he died on Father's Day, June 20, 2004, before I had a chance to meet him.

Dad and His Drums

My cousins Thaddeus and Crystal Garrison (Las Vegas February 2021)

Meeting Uncle Adrian (January 2022)

Family Group (January 2022)

Meeting my Brother Kevin for the first time in Buffalo (June 2022)

Me & Kevin at the Anchor Bar in Buffalo (June 2022)

Meeting My Family

*Cousins Glenn, Jacqueline, Illona, and My Sister Gisselle
in Texas (August 2022)*

Me & My Sister Giselle

Me & My Sister Giselle

Me at the Mary Kay Corporate Office in Dallas (2022)

WINNING BIG!!!

November 10, 2023, I won the showcase showdown on "The Price is Right" and received numerous prizes, including a hot tub, an electric bike, and a brand-new 2024 SUV.

APRIL 2024
ALL TOGETHER NOW…
FINALLY, MY CIRCLE IS COMPLETE

Margaret at Lake Shore Central High (April 2024)

Me and Margaret, Niagara Falls (April 2024)

*Me and Margaret at Margaret's surprise Birthday party
at Dave & Buster's. (April 2024)*

*Margaret with her Daughters at her surprise Birthday Party
at Dave & Buster's (Buffalo April 2024)*

My brother Kevin, my nephew Kevin, and his son (Buffalo April 2024)

Mom, Me, Julie, and Joey at Julie's Gender Reveal Party (April 2024)

Cousins Lisa and Robyn (April 2024)

Cousin Glen, Sister Giselle, Cousins Darlene, Jacqueline,
Illona and Me (Texas, April 2024)

Cousin Glen, Sister Giselle & Illona (Texas, April 2024)

Cousins Illona & Jackie (Texas, April 2024)

My Sister Giselle and Cousin Darlene – (Texas, April 2024)

About the Author

I returned to college to finish what I started in 1979. I graduated Cum Laude with an associate degree in Theater in 2019. I still love acting and have a great agent. Since relocating to Los Angeles, I have been on more than 50 shows as a background actress. I have been a contestant on the Price Is Right and Let's Make A Deal twice. I had the opportunity to perform several times on stage with military veterans. We wrote and directed our own true stories. I also had several opportunities to perform the National Anthem for a well-known yearly horse show and an Assemblyman in Los Angeles.

I am a member of The Watered Garden Fellowship Church with Pastor and Psalmist, Desmond Pringle and First Lady Tanya Love-Pringle. I first met them at an event. I admired them as a couple and how humble they continue to be. Lady Tanya invited me to a Mary Kay party, and I started my consultant business two months later.

I am an entrepreneur, working independently as a successful Mary Kay Beauty Consultant. I am also a member of Hollywood Post 43, and the NABMW (National Association of Black Military Women). I held the position of Chairwoman for four years for the Veterans Affairs Committee - Beverly Hills/Hollywood NAACP branch. I was the program manager for Arts Up LA Veterans Empowerment Theater for six years.

In 1984, while stationed in Heilbronn, West Germany I received the Best Supporting Actress Award in 7th Corps Tournament of Plays for my performance in a comedy production. I was also awarded Certificates of Appreciation from the City of Los Angeles for Contributions to Military Veterans 2017, and as a panelist for their 2018 national theme for Black History Month "African Americans in War Times: Abroad and at Home." Most recently, on November 11, 2022, the California State Assembly's "Veterans Family Reunion" and the U.S. House of Representatives presented me with a Certificate of Special Congressional Recognition from then Congresswoman Karen Bass.

Adopted, Returned, Unwanted...My Foster Care Journey is Judith Levisy's first published book.

> *Statistics say that over 40% of children in foster care will be incarcerated, homeless, on drugs, or dead within three years of leaving the system.*

www.ingramcontent.com/pod-product-compliance
Lightning Source LLC
Chambersburg PA
CBHW070818160726
48004CB00001B/327